D1123461

Team Teaching

New Pedagogies and Practices for Teaching in Higher Education series

In the same series:

Blended Learning
Across the Disciplines, Across the Academy
Edited by Francine S. Glazer

Cooperative Learning in Higher Education
Across the Disciplines, Across the Academy
Edited by Barbara J. Millis

Just-in-Time Teaching
Across the Disciplines, Across the Academy
Edited by Scott Simkins and Mark H. Maier

Published in association with The National Teaching and Learning Forum

Lesson Study
Using Classroom Inquiry to Improve Teaching and Learning in Higher Education
Bill Cerbin
Foreword by Pat Hutchings

Team Teaching

Across the Disciplines, Across the Academy

Edited by **Kathryn M. Plank**

Foreword by **James Rhem**

Published in Association with The National Teaching and Learning Forum

STERLING, VIRGINIA

COPYRIGHT © 2011 BY
STYLUS PUBLISHING, LLC.

Published by Stylus Publishing, LLC
22883 Quicksilver Drive
Sterling, Virginia 20166-2102

All rights reserved. No part of this book may be
reprinted or reproduced in any form or by any
electronic, mechanical, or other means, now known or
hereafter invented, including photocopying,
recording, and information storage and retrieval,
without permission in writing from the publisher.

Library of Congress Cataloging-in-Publication Data
Team teaching : across the disciplines, across the
academy / edited by Kathryn M. Plank ; foreword by
James Rhem.—1st ed.
    p.   cm. — (New pedagogies and practices for
teaching in higher education series)
Includes bibliographical references and index.
ISBN 978-1-57922-453-0 (cloth : alk. paper)
ISBN 978-1-57922-454-7 (pbk. : alk. paper)
ISBN 978-1-57922-717-3 (library networkable
e-edition : alk. paper)—ISBN 978-1-57922-718-0
(consumer e-edition : alk. paper)
1. Teaching teams.   2. Interdisciplinary approach in
education.   3. College teaching.   4. Education,
Higher—Curricula.   I. Plank, Kathryn M.
LB1029.T4A36   2011
378.1′25—dc23
                                                    2011017814

13-digit ISBN: 978-1-57922-453-0 (cloth)
13-digit ISBN: 978-1-57922-454-7 (paper)
13-digit ISBN: 978-1-57922-717-3 (library
networkable e-edition)
13-digit ISBN: 978-1-57922-718-0 (consumer
e-edition)

Printed in the United States of America

All first editions printed on acid free paper
that meets the American National Standards Institute
Z39-48 Standard.

Bulk Purchases

Quantity discounts are available
for use in workshops and for staff
development.
Call 1-800-232-0223

First Edition, 2011

10   9   8   7   6   5   4   3   2   1

To David, who I thought was my first student until I realized he was my greatest teacher.

Contents

Acknowledgments

For years I wished there was a book I could give faculty that not only would give practical ideas for team teaching, but also would capture some of the magic that can happen when teachers teach together. I am very grateful to James Rhem for giving me the opportunity to create just such a book. I knew from our first conversation, when we talked about how powerful our own team-teaching experiences had been, that we shared a vision for what this book could be. I'm thankful for James's support and patience throughout this project, and for Susan Slesinger's editing expertise and help from the staff at Stylus.

This book exists because of the teachers who contributed chapters. I'm grateful that this project gave me the opportunity to talk with them, to learn from them, and to share their stories with others. They are truly inspirational. In a time when many question the teaching and learning that happens on our college campuses, I know from my work as an educational developer that there are so many dedicated college teachers out there creating transformative learning experiences for their students and often with little recognition. I am thrilled that this book gives us the opportunity to learn from a few of those teachers.

I would also like to thank everyone I have ever taught with, including my colleagues from the University Center for the Advancement of Teaching at The Ohio State University: Alan Kalish, Stephanie Rohdieck, Teresa Johnson, Laurie Maynell, and Gerald Nelms. I'd also like to thank colleagues from the Professional and Organizational Development (POD) Network with whom I have copresented and from whom I have learned so much, including Michele DiPietro, Peter Felten, Deandra Little, Shaun Longstreet, and Laurel Willingham-McLain. And I must thank my students, who team teach the course with me and make me a better teacher each time they do so.

I am thankful for my family, who are all, in one way or the other, responsible for my love of teaching: William, Dorothy, and David Plank; Carol, David, Kristina, and Melanie Crawford; and Paul and Darcy Granello. Finally, my deepest gratitude goes to Melissa Leeper for supporting me in everything I do and bringing joy to every day of our lives.

Foreword

Not that long ago, the word *pedagogy* didn't occur that often in faculty conversations about teaching. Today, one hears it frequently. Without putting too much weight on the prominence of a single word, subtle shifts in discourse, in vocabulary, often do mark significant shifts in thinking, and faculty thinking about teaching has changed over the last several decades. Faculty have always wanted to teach well, wanted their students to learn and succeed, but for a very long time faculty have taught as they were taught, and for the students who were like them in temperament and intelligence, the approach worked well enough. When only a highly filtered population of students sought higher education, the need to look beyond those approaches to teaching lay dormant. When a much larger and more diverse population began enrolling, the limits of traditional teaching emerged more sharply.

At the same time, intelligence itself became a more deeply understood phenomenon. Recognition of multiple kinds of intelligence—visual, auditory, kinesthetic, etc. (Gardner, 1983)—found wide acceptance, as did different styles of learning even within those different kinds of intelligence (Myers-Briggs, among others). Efforts to build ever more effective "thinking machines," that is, computers, through artificial intelligence sharpened understanding of how information needed to be processed for it to be assembled and used effectively. The seminal article, "Cognitive Apprenticeship: Teaching the Craft of Reading, Writing and Mathematics" (Collins, Brown, & Newman, 1989), was one by-product of this research, and one instructive aspect of this work was how it looked back to accumulated wisdom to lay its foundations for moving forward. Public schools had long dealt with large, diverse populations rather than highly filtered ones. Teachers there understood terms such as *scaffolding, wait time,* and *chunking* in conscious ways that were new to those at more advanced levels in education. Now, many of these terms and, more important, these conscious and deliberate ways of thinking about teaching, have become commonplace in higher education.

Even more recently all this work has found support and expansion in neurobiological research into the human brain and how it operates, and in the study of groups and how they operate.

If renewed attention to teaching in higher education began as something of a "fix-it" shop approach to help individual faculty having problems with their teaching, it didn't stay that way very long. As Gaff and Simpson (1994) detail in their history of faculty development in the United States, pressure from the burgeoning "baby boom" population brought the whole business of university teaching up for reconsideration. What was relevance? What were appropriate educational goals, and what were the most effective means of meeting them? Traditionally, faculty primarily were expected to remain current in their fields of expertise. Now, a whole new set of still-forming expectations has begun to spring up on campuses all over the country.

Change often fails to come easily and smoothly. Generational and social conflicts, together with passionate political conflicts focusing on the unpopular war in Vietnam, may have fueled the pressure for changes in teaching while making such changes more conflict-ridden than they needed to be. It is important to remember that faculty have always wanted to teach well and see their students succeed. As the clouds of conflict of those decades have passed, the intellectual fruits have remained and grown. Some ascribe credit for change in faculty attitudes toward teaching to the social pressures of those decades. Whatever truth lies in that ascription, it seems equally clear that faculty's innate intellectual curiosity and eagerness to succeed in their life's work deserve as much credit, certainly in today's interest in improved teaching.

Faculty face a challenge in embracing new understandings of effective teaching not unlike the challenge of any population of diverse intelligences in learning and applying new information. Some understanding emerging in the 1980s (in which much of the new thinking on teaching and learning began to appear) has cross-disciplinary, universal applicability—as evidenced, for example, in "Seven Principles of Good Practice in Higher Education" (Chickering & Gamson, 1987). But just as diverse people learn in diverse ways, diverse faculty will apply even universal principles in different ways, since both personalities and disciplinary cultures vary. Perhaps that is why many pedagogical insights into effective teaching have not aggregated into one universal, best way to teach. Instead the inquiry into effective teaching has spawned a variety of pedagogical approaches, each with strengths appropriate to particular teaching styles and situations.

While faculty today have greater curiosity about new understandings of effective ways to teach, they remain as cautious as anyone else about change.

If they teach biology, they wonder how a particular approach might play out in teaching biology rather than how it works in teaching English literature. If they teach English literature, they may wonder if problem-based teaching (a highly effective approach in the sciences) has anything to offer their teaching and whether anyone in their discipline has tried it. Every new idea requires translation and receives it in the hands of the next person to take it up and apply it. And this is as it should be. Thus, this series of books strives to give faculty examples of new approaches to teaching as they are being applied in a representative sample of academic disciplines. In doing so, it extends the basic idea of *The National Teaching and Learning FORUM*. For roughly 20 years, the central goal of *FORUM* has been to offer faculty ideas in context—that is, to present them enough theory so that whatever idea about teaching and learning being discussed makes sense intellectually, and then to present that idea in an applied context. From this combination faculty can see how an approach might fit in their own practice. Faculty do not need formulae; they need only to see ideas in contexts. They'll take it from there. And so our series of books offers faculty a multipaned window into a variety of nontraditional pedagogical approaches now being applied with success in different higher education disciplines. Faculty will look in and find something of value for their own teaching. As I've said and believe with all my heart, faculty have always wanted to teach well and see their students succeed.

I'm especially pleased to have a book on team teaching in the series. I've told this story many times, but it bears repeating. I became deeply, even passionately, convinced of the value of team teaching years ago while leading a discussion of *Huckleberry Finn*. As it happens, my old college roommate, a professor of English, was visiting and sitting in on the class. At one point, he just joined the discussion, addressing me by name with his comment. Instantly, and I mean instantly, the affect and attention in the room changed. Students seemed stunned to see two adults interested in the material enough to have different points of view and urgent questions about it. They wanted to be part of this conversation. They could see that we really were having a discussion, that this was an adventure they could join and be seen as respected fellow travelers. Having two faculty there, taking the material and each other's differing points of view seriously, made all the difference.

Sadly, administrative worries and money often hamper team teaching, but, as Kathryn Plank has found, there are campuses where the transformative power and, hence, value of team teaching have been recognized, so ways have been found to surmount those barriers. I can only hope that readers of this volume will find ways to bring team teaching to their campuses. I have never felt more alive in my teaching than I did that afternoon years ago discussing *Huckleberry Finn*.

—James Rhem
Executive Editor,
The National Teaching and Learning FORUM

REFERENCES

Chickering, A., & Gamson, Z. (1987, March). Seven principles of good practice in higher education. *AAHE Bulletin*, 3–7.

Collins, A., Brown, J. S., & Newman, S. E. (1989). Cognitive apprenticeship: Teaching the craft of reading, writing and mathematics. In L. B. Resnick (Ed.), *Knowing, learning and instruction: Essays in honor of Robert Glaser* (pp. 453–494). Hillsdale, NJ: Erlbaum.

Gaff, J. G., & Simpson, R. D. (1994, Spring). Faculty development in the United States. *Innovative Higher Education, 18*(3), 167–176.

Gardner, H. (1983). *The theory of multiple intelligences.* New York: Basic Books.

Introduction

Kathryn M. Plank

Team teaching can be wonderful, as both faculty and students are "surprised by joy" when they make hitherto unseen connections and experience the lovely rigor of intellectual activity. (Rinn & Weir, 1984, p. 10)

When I first began talking about this book with James Rhem, the series editor, we quickly discovered a mutual enthusiasm for team teaching. We had both, as teachers, felt the joy that Rinn and Weir (1984) describe in the introductory quote. Our excitement for the topic encouraged us to produce a volume that would capture some of the joy of intellectual discovery and community that can emerge in the team-taught classroom.

In the following months, as I talked with the authors of the book's chapters—all of whom have taught as part of a team—I was again struck by the excitement they shared. For them, the team-teaching experience was clearly more than just a teaching method. These teachers talked about their classes as scholarly communities in which teachers and students worked together to understand important ideas. They described how the students weren't just learning content, but were beginning to understand how we know that content. They delighted in the new territory opened up by breaking down traditional disciplinary boundaries, and they reflected on how having more than one teacher in the classroom led naturally to dialogue and active learning.

As I listened, I could not help but notice that they were talking about not only what students gained from the experience, what students learned, and how students changed. They were just as—if not more—excited to talk about how the experience changed them. None of them claimed that team teaching was easy or saved time (in fact, the opposite was almost always true), but it was very clear that the rewards of team teaching make the time and effort more than worth it. Team teaching took them out of their standard classes and teaching styles and thrust them into unfamiliar territory where they had to master new material, negotiate with others, and trust their colleagues. The payoff was that they learned new things about the subject matter, about their colleagues, and about themselves as teachers.

The goal of this book is to explore the dynamic that occurs when multiple teachers grapple together with course content and thus open up courses for the students to join in their exploration. For that reason, the examples are all courses in which two or more instructors work collaboratively to plan, teach, and assess a course. While at first glance it may seem that team teaching is simply a way to divide labor, at its best it can enrich the process of learning for both students and faculty.

Each of the five essays in this book shares the story of a course at a different institution. The chapters provide examples that reflect a number of different variables in team-taught courses. First, they represent courses in a variety of different disciplines, including sciences, social sciences, humanities, and the arts, and at a range of course levels, from first-year seminars to graduate courses. Second, they demonstrate a number of different models for instructional teams, such as faculty from the same disciplines, from related disciplines, from two very different disciplines, from different institutions, and one pairing of a faculty member and a staff member. Finally, the first four cases are co-authored by pairs of faculty who have team taught recent and/or ongoing courses, and are thus the products of teams still close to the experience. The last case study is a look back by one teacher at a course taught over a decade ago that reflects on what worked, why it ended, and how a course like it might work in the future.

Together these chapters give insight into the impact of team teaching on student learning and faculty development. They also reveal the challenges, both pedagogical and administrative, that make team teaching work.

TEAM TEACHING AND STUDENT LEARNING: A ROUGH-AND-TUMBLE ENTERPRISE

> Our knowledge of the world comes from gathering around great things in a complex and interactive community of truth. But good teachers do more than deliver the news from that community to their students. Good teachers replicate the process of knowing by engaging students in the dynamics of the community of truth. (Palmer, 1998, p. 115)

There's a messiness to team teaching that presents some of its biggest challenges, but also some of its most promising opportunities. Team teaching moves beyond the familiar and predictable and creates an environment of uncertainty, dialogue, and discovery. And that is what learning is all about.

Whether one is looking at classifications of critical thinking, or definitions of deep approaches to learning, or models of cognitive and ethical development (see Anderson & Krathwohl, 2001; Bowden & Marton, 2004; Perry, 1968), the goal for student learning is a dynamic, complex, and often unsettling place. In reporting on his study of what the best college teachers do, Ken Bain (2004) says, "[P]eople learn by confronting intriguing, beautiful, or important problems, authentic tasks that will challenge them to grapple with ideas, rethink their assumptions, and examine their mental models of reality" (p. 18).

Team teaching in itself is not really a teaching method and will not make achieving these learning goals inevitable. The instructors must still design a course and implement methods that challenge students to "grapple with ideas" and "rethink their assumptions." But team teaching does provide an ideal environment for this type of engagement, in part by making it almost impossible to stick with a teacher-centered classroom in which the teacher is the sole authority delivering knowledge to the students. The interaction of two teachers—both the intellectual interaction involved in the design of the course and the pedagogical interaction in teaching the course—creates a dynamic environment that reflects the way scholars make meaning of the world.

Almost by definition, team teaching encourages students (and teachers) to view the subject matter from multiple perspectives. When multiple teachers represent multiple perspectives on course content, they move students away from dualistic thinking toward higher (and deeper) stages of cognitive and ethical development. Students who enter a course wanting to see the teacher as the source of the "right" answers are now confronted with two or more teachers who have different views and sometimes completely different methodologies. While this may create some anxiety for students, as we discuss later, it also models for them how different perspectives come together to construct meaning.

Perhaps the clearest example of multiple perspectives comes in a common model of team teaching: the interdisciplinary course in which faculty from different disciplines teach around a common topic or theme. The next two chapters of this book explore two such courses. In chapter 1, Amy Jessen-Marshall and Hal Lescinsky, a microbiologist and a paleontologist, respectively, at Otterbein University, talk about their course, "Origins," which uses the techniques and perspectives of two different science disciplines to examine the question of human origins and evolution. In chapter 2, Min-Ken Liao and Sarah Worth of Furman University describe their course, "Disease and Culture," which examines the social, cultural, and ethical impact of disease from the divergent perspectives of philosophy and biology. As Liao and Worth say, "We believe this type of collaborative and interdisciplinary interaction in and of itself is a powerful demonstration to students that focused, interdisciplinary, team approaches to the pursuit of knowledge are at the core of a liberal arts education."

If it is true that "the undergraduate experience, often criticized as being fragmented, is challenged to develop more coherence by introducing students to essential knowledge, to connections across the disciplines, and to the application of knowledge to life beyond the campus" (McDaniel & Colarulli, 1997, p. 19), then higher education has been responding with greater emphasis on working across disciplinary boundaries. Both of these courses are products of initiatives intentionally designed to promote greater interdisciplinarity. "Origins" is part of Otterbein's Integrative Studies Program, a core element of the university's liberal arts mission, which "aims to prepare Otterbein undergraduates for the challenges and complexity of a 21st century world" by emphasizing "interdisciplinary and integrative skills, competencies, and ways of knowing" (http://www.otterbein.edu/is/). Likewise, Furman's general education program brings "a greater variety of intellectual perspectives into meaningful dialogue with one another, thus highlighting for students both the complementarity and the uniqueness of departmental and disciplinary voices" (*Invigorating Intellectual Life*, 2005).

This interplay of disciplinary voices is also evident in an introductory science course offered in the 1990s at Indiana University–Purdue University Fort Wayne (described in chapter 5). In this course, taught by Ronald Duchovic and a team of faculty from different disciplines in the sciences, "it quickly became obvious that each question raised in the class discussion can be examined from the perspective of multiple, discipline-specific paradigms." The goal was to help students see the nature of scientific thinking and begin to understand how scientists make sense of the world.

Seeing differences between different perspectives is an important first step for students, but perhaps even more important is for them to see the connections. For example, Jessen-Marshall and Lescinsky describe how in their "Origins" class, "students will see how different fields address common questions, using a variety of techniques that support the validity of scientific tenets. This interconnectedness, often underappreciated by nonscientists, is in large part what gives scientists confidence that their understanding is correct." In a time when scientific literacy is becoming more important, classes such as these can contribute to students' becoming more knowledgeable citizens.

What these teachers are observing is a model of cognitive apprenticeship. Team teaching can "provide a means of focusing more on the process of learning instead of only on accumulating content knowledge" (Shibley, 2006, p. 271). Or, as Duchovic says of his course, students get to "hear a scientist think." When multiple instructors engage with each other in the class, they make their thinking processes and intellectual frameworks visible, thus encouraging greater metacognition on the part of the students, and better understanding of how we know what we know.

While interdisciplinary teams are one way to encourage this focus on process, it works for other kinds of partnerships as well. In chapter 3, Robert Richter and Margaret Thomas of Connecticut College bring together two very different sets of professional experience to the course "Arts and Community." Richter, who holds a staff position in arts programming, and Thomas, a faculty member in music theory, use the interplay of their two roles to model the concept of community that is central to the course topic.

Demonstrating yet another configuration, Mathew Ouellett and Edith Fraser discuss in chapter 4 how an interracial team of teachers from different institutions can facilitate students' understanding of race and racism in social work in their course, "Racism in the United States: Implications for Social Work Practice," in part by having a team of teachers "modeling authentic collaboration across racial differences." As Ouellett and Fraser say, "Perhaps the most unanticipated outcome of our teaching has been the discovery that, from our students' perspectives, observing our daily interactions and relationship as colleagues was more important to their learning than the formal curriculum."

In modeling the scholarly and professional processes of their fields, these teams of teachers can also create a learning environment where it is safe for students to confront intimidating subjects like science or challenging topics like racism. Seeing their teachers learn from each other and even disagree with each other models for students how scholars and informed citizens within a community of learning can navigate a complex and uncertain world.

Of course, none of this happens automatically. For example, although Jessen-Marshall and Lescinsky constructed their course to have pairs of labs exploring related topics from two different disciplinary approaches, the connection between the labs that was so apparent to them was at first lost on the students. They learned that they needed to make the connections clearer and more explicit for students, even to the point of renaming the two different labs part 1 and part 2 of the same lab to reinforce the connections.

Similarly, just watching teachers interact is not enough. I once took a class as a student in which team teaching consisted mainly of four teachers arguing with each other in front of an audience of befuddled students. The teachers may have enjoyed the intellectual interplay of different disciplinary paradigms, but they apparently forgot that novice learners do not always see or understand the structure of content knowledge enough to appreciate this kind of dialogue.

In contrast, the classes described in this book all use many reflective activities—journals, reflection papers, guided discussion—to help students see the connections and grapple with complex and conflicting ideas. The combination of modeling reflection for the students and having students engage in their own reflection provides the kind of cognitive apprenticeship that introduces students into a community of learning.

As the Furman University curriculum review committee states, "Stimulating the mind for the pursuit of knowledge [is] a rough-and-tumble enterprise" (*Invigorating*, p. 9). Learning is indeed a rough-and-tumble enterprise, and so is team teaching. But team teaching can also create an environment that makes this exploration safe. One method is to work actively to build community in the class. For example, Richter and Thomas's class attended arts performances together, and Liao and Worth's students bonded by baking cookies together to raise money for mosquito nets in Africa. But it also helps for students to see their teachers learning and questioning.

TEAM TEACHING AND FACULTY DEVELOPMENT

> Talking to colleagues about what we do unravels the shroud of silence in which our practice is wrapped. (Brookfield, 1995, p. 35)

Students aren't the only ones grappling with the learning process in the team-taught classroom. The faculty in the room are exploring, discovering, and taking risks right alongside them.

If better and deeper learning is the primary goal of team-taught classes, a valuable side benefit is the growth and development of faculty as teachers. The impact on faculty development has been a large part of the scholarship on team teaching. In interviews with faculty who had team taught, Davis (1997) found them commenting on both the new knowledge they had gained and how much they had learned about teaching (p. 121). Shibley (2006) also discovered from his own multiple experiences in team teaching that it "provides an opportunity for colleagues to model learning for students because in the best team teaching experiences, colleagues continue to learn from each other, about both content and teaching" (p. 271). Robinson and Schaible (1995) attribute these gains to collaboration that encourages partners to experiment with new ideas and give feedback to each other on pedagogical practices (p. 59).

The authors in this book describe the learning that takes place in the team-teaching setting—learning of both content and teaching. And while it is as much a struggle for them sometimes as it is for students, the rewards may be even greater.

In some cases, the authors literally took on the role of student. Jessen-Marshall and Lescinsky, who teach the Origins course at Otterbein, took each other's labs, which pushed them out of their comfort zone, but helped them understand more fully the very connections they were teaching. They also attended together a course offered by the National Science Foundation on how to teach evolution.

Likewise, Worth and Liao attended each other's classes at Furman University before teaching together, even though neither had recent (or necessarily positive) experience in the other's field. Their experience helped them appreciate what the students would soon discover: that confronting different ways of knowing can cause anxiety. Their goal was not only to increase student learning, but also to "change the way we teach our own course and conduct our own scholarly activities in the future."

In a slightly different scenario, Richter and Thomas found that their Art and Community course at Connecticut College was a topic tangential to both of their areas of interest, so they needed to learn more about it, exploring the issues and finding readings, engaging in what they call a kind of professional development. And Ronald Duchovic reflects on how teaching with faculty from other disciplines forces one outside one's own framework for viewing the world.

Teams also report learning more about teaching. Much of faculty development is about helping teachers reflect on why they teach the way they do, how to assess what is working, and what other options are available. By opening the door of the classroom to a second teacher, team teaching has a built-in teaching development system. As Ouellett and Fraser discovered in their social work course, teams can "provide each other mentoring, feedback, and fresh perspective on student interaction."

But again, this does not happen automatically. All of the authors stress the importance of working together at all stages of the process, from the initial planning through the final assessment. They also built in ways to meet regularly. Richter and Thomas, for example, scheduled a weekly meeting after each class period to review the class that just happened and prepare for the next. Ouellett and Fraser not only met weekly, but they also were able to participate in a luncheon series sponsored by the program that runs their course as well as celebratory functions at the end of the term.

Some of the pairs also describe switching off teaching and taking the lead in a class on the other person's area of expertise, in part to broaden their own skills, but also to signal to students that they were teaching as a true team, not as alternating experts.

All of the authors warn that team teaching is not half the work of an individual course, and, in fact, is usually more work than solo teaching. When we teach our own classes, especially ones we have taught before, it's possible to cut corners, to take shortcuts, to "wing it." When we share the class with another teacher, we cannot do that. We need to be prepared not only for what we're going to do, but also for all of the possible ways in which our teaching may interact with another's.

Worth and Liao describe how just as the interdisciplinary nature of their course made more visible for students how they learn, it also made more visible for them as teachers how they teach. They had to negotiate disciplinary differences in assignments and teaching methods, but doing so expanded their individual repertoires and made them more reflective of their own choices.

Perhaps the simplest way to state the impact of team teaching on faculty development is Amy Jessen-Marshall's reflection: "I truly believe I've become a better teacher for having taught repeatedly with Dr. Lescinsky." Any educational development program would be thrilled with such a result.

PEDAGOGICAL AND ADMINISTRATIVE CHALLENGES TO TEAM TEACHING

While I may seem to be offering team teaching as the solution to all of higher education's problems, neither I nor the authors in this book are making that claim. Team teaching has some obvious and significant challenges.

Some of those discussed in the chapters that follow are pedagogical issues. Perhaps the most frequent challenge discussed is the difficulty of grading and grading expectations. While team teachers celebrate the value of multiple perspectives, they also learn that multiple expectations can be confusing and anxiety-inducing for students. Who will grade what? Using what criteria? Liao and Worth, for example, found that a discussion of passive voice that was intended to introduce students to disciplinary standards of writing only made students worry that they could never please both teachers simultaneously, even though their individual grades were very consistent. One solution Richter and Thomas worked out was to have both teachers read everything, even if one had primary responsibility for grading a particular assignment. With this system, students recognized that both teachers were the audience for their work, so they didn't have to wonder which one to try to please.

Grading anxiety is part of a bigger challenge that comes from having more than one authority figure in the room. Several of the pairs observe that students were not always sure who was "in charge"; some even say that students would try to play one teacher off the other and set them up in contrary positions. All of the authors emphasize the need to work together to develop a shared responsibility and vision and to make clear to students that they were working as a unified team. Sometimes they did this by meeting with students together in office hours. Richter and Thomas discovered it was useful to confront the issue explicitly on the first day and tell students, "We are in daily contact with each other; you may direct questions to either one of us, and we may well consult with the other about your questions." The dispersed authority of the team-taught classroom may be new to students, but it can help direct them away from the dualistic thinking that leads them to assume an external authority.

The pedagogical challenges of team teaching are not unlike the challenges that come with any other teaching method. Perhaps the more distinctive obstacles are the administrative and structural challenges that come with having two faculty, often from different departments, in the same classroom. In today's climate of budget cuts and fiscal accountability, concerns about paying two people to do a job traditionally done by one are not trivial. In fact, for some it may seem an unaffordable luxury. But, considering the student learning and faculty development opportunities of team teaching, one might ask if we can afford not to. As McDaniel and Colarulli (1997) encourage, we must look at short-term versus long-term productivity.

Many administrative decisions made with the goal of short-term productivity—increasing class size, for example, or increasing the number of courses taught by part-time faculty—may work against our long-term institutional goals. They can be a false efficiency. In fact, McDaniel and Colarulli (1997) claim:

> Many short-term productivity considerations are in the longer term self-destructive for an institution. . . . In general, larger and larger classes, fewer full-time faculty, and more part-time faculty mean less interaction for students with faculty, in and out of the classroom, and with each other. These choices mean

that innovation and curricular change are less likely to happen as full-time faculty have less and less time and energy to invest in change. (p. 29)

If we look at long-term costs, they depend more on reputation and retention (of both faculty and students). These measures support the investment in team-taught and interdisciplinary courses. Assessment for accreditation increasingly looks at evidence of student learning outcomes. Instruments like the National Survey of Student Engagement (NSSE) assess universities using categories such as active and collaborative learning and student-faculty interaction, which are achieved more through methods such as team teaching than by increasing class size.

For many universities, the goals of team teaching are closely aligned with institutional goals. For the liberal arts colleges in this book, recruiting students depends on convincing them of the value of a liberal education, and team-taught courses like those described here are a concrete example of the values of liberal education in practice.

Faculty development also has long-term costs and impacts. Retaining faculty and keeping them as productive teachers benefits an institution. Opportunities to grow and refresh one's skills at mid-career, and to reflect on and change one's teaching, can lead to renewed job satisfaction and greater long-term productivity. Occasional team teaching might be one method to reinvigorate a faculty member's career.

Yet, while long-term productivity may be our focus, the very real question of short-term funding still remains. It's not surprising, perhaps, that several of the courses in this book were started with grant funds. Many funding agencies, such as the National Science Foundation (NSF) and the National Endowment for the Humanities (NEH), offer grants for interdisciplinary and team-taught courses that can be used to start up a team teaching program.

Other internal changes might also make the courses possible. In the example at Otterbein, the university decided to raise the enrollment for the course when it moved to team teaching, so the costs were minimal.

McDaniel and Colarulli (1997) offer an alternative model for team teaching, the "dispersed team model," which also allows a course to reach a greater number of students. In this model, a team of faculty designs an interdisciplinary course, but the course is then divided into sections. The entire class meets once a week with all of the teachers present, but then for the other class meetings, each faculty member teaches only one section of students.

As part of the same program in which Liao and Worth teach, Furman University is experimenting with just such a dispersed model, which it calls *clustering.* The course, "Mars: Shoulder of Giants," was designed by a team of faculty from different disciplines and originally taught in the full team-teaching model with all faculty attending all class sessions. However, in part because of faculty workload concerns, it will now be taught in separate sections by different teachers, but all of the groups will meet together once a week for labs (personal communication with Mike Winiski, November 2, 2010). This model allows a school to maintain a student-teacher ratio similar to what it would be without team teaching, but still benefits from faculty collaboration in designing and teaching the course.

As Ronald Duchovic explores in chapter 5, there are also possibilities in using technology. For example, faculty at different schools can now design a course together, teach it at their own institutions, but then meet as a group through either synchronous (for example, teleconferencing) or asynchronous (for example, blogging, online discussion) communications.

Models such as these can help alleviate some of the costs of team teaching, but still maintain the layers of collaboration needed to create a course that is truly a community of learning.

Finally, one must also remember that no one is suggesting all courses be converted to team teaching. For many teachers—and students—a team-taught class is a valuable opportunity, but not one that would work all the time for every course. It requires of both teachers and students an intense investment of time and effort that might be hard to sustain, but that has profound and meaningful rewards.

Over the past 20 years, many of the innovations and trends in higher education have been built on the value of community. Emphasis on active and collaborative learning (Barr & Tagg, 1995; Bonwell & Eison, 1991) is based on the idea that students learn better in community. Initiatives like the Scholarship of Teaching & Learning (SoTL) and faculty learning communities rest on the principle that college faculty are part of a larger community of teachers who can learn from each other. And the focus on interdisciplinarity is founded on the principle that knowledge is not naturally segregated into silos but is part of what Palmer (1998) calls a "complex and interactive community of truth" (p. 115).

Perhaps no teaching method embodies all aspects of this community better than team teaching. At its best, team teaching creates a community for better student learning, a community for faculty to learn from each other, and a community of knowledge that transcends disciplinary ways of knowing.

The chapters that follow share some of the joys of team teaching as well as the challenges. These five teams of faculty prove that team teaching is not only a rewarding experience for teachers but also an exciting opportunity to achieve our highest goals in education.

REFERENCES

Anderson, L. W., & Krathwohl, D. R. (Eds.). (2001). *A taxonomy for learning, teaching and assessing: A revision of Bloom's Taxonomy of educational objectives.* New York: Longman.

Bain, K. (2004). *What the best college teachers do.* Cambridge, MA: Harvard University Press.

Barr, R. B., & Tagg, J. (1995, November/December). A new paradigm for undergraduate education. *Change, 27*(6), 13–25.

Bonwell, C. C., & Eison, J. A. (1991). *Active learning: Creating excitement in the classroom* (ASHE-ERIC Higher Education Report No. 1, 1991). Washington, DC: George Washington University Clearinghouse on Higher Education.

Bowden, J., & Marton, F. (2004). *The university of learning: Beyond quality and competence.* London: Routledge.

Brookfield, S. D. (1995). *Becoming a critically reflective teacher.* San Francisco: Jossey-Bass.

Davis, J. R. (1997). *Interdisciplinary courses and team teaching.* Phoenix, AZ: Oryx Press.

Invigorating intellectual life: A proposal for Furman University's academic program and calendar. (2005, September 10). Report to the Furman Faculty from the Curriculum Review Committee.

McDaniel, E. A., & Colarulli, G. C. (1997). Collaborative teaching in the face of productivity concerns: The dispersed team model. *Innovative Higher Education, 22* (1), 19–36.

Palmer, P. J. (1998). *The courage to teach: Exploring the inner landscape of a teacher's life.* San Francisco: Jossey-Bass.

Perry, W. (1968). *Forms of intellectual and ethical development in the college years.* New York: Holt, Rinehart, & Winston.

Rinn, F. J., & Weir, S. B. (1984). Former champ makes comeback: Yea, team. *Improving College and University Teaching, 32*(1), 5–10.

Robinson, B., & Schaible, R. M. (1995). Collaborative teaching: Reaping the benefits. *College Teaching, 43*(2), 57–59.

Shibley, I. A. (2006). Interdisciplinary team teaching: Negotiating pedagogical differences. *College Teaching, 54*(3), 271–274.

1

Origins

Team Teaching in the Sciences

Amy Jessen-Marshall and Halard L. Lescinsky

Because this course deals with a broad range of scientific fields, having it team taught by members with different specialties made the material more cohesive.

It was hard because it felt like two different classes. Almost 2 different subjects to learn. They didn't blend together for me.

This approach made it hard for me because I didn't see how one professor's lessons had much to do with the other's.

These two professors complement each other quite well. They're great people and great instructors. We not only as students learn from them, but they also learn from each other. This allows this course to cover lots of ground in many areas.

Selected student reflections on "Origins," a sophomore-level Integrative Studies science course for all students, 2004–2009

CONTEXT FOR DEVELOPMENT FOR TEAM-TAUGHT INTERDISCIPLINARY COURSES AT OTTERBEIN

As is apparent in the student reflections above, and after teaching five sections of our Origins course together since 2004, we have come to expect that for some students this multidisciplinary, interdisciplinary experience works well for student learning. For some students the experience of having two instructors, who practice science in different fields of study, paleontology and molecular microbiology, respectively, and who have different personalities and sometimes different views on pedagogy, will lead them to insights into how science is conducted, the challenges of asking good questions and designing good experiments, and, ultimately, the value of how different fields of research can and do contribute to a larger understanding of the world we inhabit and the theories and laws scientists elucidate to explain it. And then again, sometimes, students just don't connect.

But that doesn't mean we don't keep trying to refine the course, develop new labs, and change the order of what we teach and even who teaches it, witnessing our own evolution in teaching our course on origins and evolution. Since introducing our course six years ago, we have had the benefit of numerous opportunities to develop, refine, and evaluate our experiences. In this chapter we share the origins of our "Origins" course, the context for why we tackled team teaching in the sciences at Otterbein, and the multiple opportunities for course development, including jointly attending a Chautauqua course on teaching evolution and seeking NSF funding for curriculum support. Over time we developed together labs that had stronger crossover, paired lectures with overlapping themes, and synthesis in class discussions. We've also done considerable assessment of not only our course but all team-taught courses we offer in the science curriculum, and we finally offer our individual insights into why we think team teaching sometimes works and sometimes really doesn't. It all comes down to organizational strategies, commitment, and personalities, with a heavy dose of patience and understanding.

Through our funding by NSF (Grant Award 0536681) as part of a larger science initiative to develop team-taught courses in the sciences, we used pre- and post-tests throughout the years of course development and implementation to ask questions about students' understanding and application of science methodology, the value of science in society, and, ultimately, on the students' experience in team-taught courses. What we've seen in the years we've taught the course is an increasingly positive trend that our partnership in the classroom makes a difference in students' understanding and appreciation of science, in particular, how many fields of science intersect to produce well-substantiated theories, like the theory of evolution.

The project started in 2003, when the science faculty at Otterbein committed to revise the contribution we made to our Integrative Studies program, which serves as our core liberal arts curriculum for all Otterbein students. At the beginning of this curriculum development, all students were required to take two Integrative Studies science courses from a menu of choices. The courses were large, comprising upwards of 70 students, predominantly lecture-based, and taken in the junior or senior year. Recognizing the limitations of this model, we looked to shift our curriculum and to reflect best practices in innovative science pedagogy. Encouraged by the chair of the Integrative Studies program, we begin to articulate the team-taught structures for the courses informed and supported by the college's commitment to the value of team teaching. Our Senior-Year Experience program had already been established and had been using team-taught courses for more than 15 years.

The development of our new team-taught curriculum was grounded in fundamental questions of how and why students learn or don't learn scientific reasoning. We began by questioning our own curricular structure. Why were our courses taught in the junior and senior year; what message did that send to students who were not majors in science disciplines? There seemed to be this perception that science was too hard. Too hard to tackle until you were an upper-class student, too challenging for students until they developed the skills that came with a liberal arts education in the first few years of college. This was an old argument, but one that no one within our curriculum had questioned in years. Was science really harder to learn than other subjects? Was Einstein really more challenging than Samuel Clemens? Where did that perception come from? Attempting to decipher the mathematical equations that underpin physics, the statistics that ground classical Mendelian genetics, or the atomic structures that inform chemistry from a science textbook can certainly induce a fair amount of stress in a student who doesn't regularly engage with these topics, but is it really true that these subjects are "harder" to learn than others?

Scientists as a group are fairly analytical and driven to analyze; as a result a significant amount of research has been done on why students perceive science as an unbreachable wall. Sheila Tobias (1985, 1990) has written since the 1980s about students' anxiety/avoidance/phobia of science, especially concerning math. Bower (2001) even noted that math phobia alone can subtract from memory and learning.

But even beyond the anxiety students bring to the classroom, additional disconnects often hinder students' success. For example, students often bring misperceptions about science into the classroom. They tend to approach science as a fact-based field to be memorized and in a language that is foreign. It's often content and not process that is stressed. One way of challenging this misperception is by engaging students in the hands-on practice of science that laboratory experiences can offer. In her book, *Innovations in Interdisciplinary Teaching*, Haynes (2002) advocates for the importance of stressing process and helping students to understand that science is a way of knowing and understanding the world.

In addition students tend to bring information from earlier experiences into the classroom, making it very difficult to "unlearn," which can set up roadblocks to accepting different information (Michael, 2002; Modell, Michael, & Wenderoth, 2005). For example, we find in our classroom that many students perceive evolution and natural selection as "survival of the fittest" when we do a pre-assessment of their understanding of evolutionary theory. Backing up to undo this preconception takes considerable effort. And finally, students bring different skills and histories to the classroom. In *Classroom Research* (1996), Cross and Steadman's discussion about students' prerequisite knowledge and learning strategies points out that students may be quite successful in one discipline, yet lack the skills to cross that divide into a different discipline.

This raises the very important point that it is not that general concepts in science are "harder" than other subjects; it's that science is "different" from other subjects. And students may not have the skill set, or the mindset, to see that difference. They get trapped in memorizing unrelated facts, they fear the use of math, and they set themselves up for frustration.

As a result the science faculty reevaluated our Integrative Studies science curriculum and established a set of learning goals for our courses, a primary focus of which would be integrative, interdisciplinary perspectives, which would present an opportunity for team-teaching.

Our goals were identified as:

1. Introduce science into the Integrative Studies curriculum earlier. (Move one required course to the sophomore year.)
   Rationale: Reduce science anxiety by modeling that science is not so "hard" that a student can't handle learning college science until his or her upper-level years.
2. Introduce hands-on, active learning into each course through lab experiences.
   Rationale: To refocus student learning from fact-based science to the *method* of science, focusing on the principles of scientific inquiry.
3. Team teach courses with faculty from different scientific disciplines.
   Rationale: Model how the scientific disciplines approach related problems from different perspectives and with different techniques. We want our students to discover that science method is universal, and that scientific theories are even stronger when evidence is available from several fields of study.

CLASS-SPECIFIC HISTORY: DEVELOPMENT OF "ORIGINS"

With these goals in mind, we set out to develop the first of the team-taught courses in the science curriculum: "Origins," to be developed by Hal Lescinsky, earth science and paleontology, and Amy Jessen-Marshall, molecular biology and microbiology. Several notable opportunities arose, which led to the success of this course.

In the spring of 2004, the National Science Foundation offered a two-day intensive course through its Chautauqua series on how to teach evolution. Until this point, we had very different experiences in teaching the theory of evolution. Hal had attended an earlier Chautauqua taught by Craig Nelson, a respected national leader in evolution pedagogy, and had accumulated a number of excellent strategies for teaching evolution. In contrast, Amy had faced serious challenges in her classroom related to teaching evolution, so she felt more trepidation about tackling the political and religious challenges of teaching evolution.

Attending the two-day course together provided us with a unique opportunity, under the guidance of an independent faculty facilitating the course, to process how to organize and strategize the first course offering together. Walking away from the course with a shared vocabulary, shared materials, and the opportunity to have been students together established an important working relationship for the development of the course. Shared faculty development was key to our team.

Having launched the course in spring 2004, and then repeating it again in fall 2004, we had back-to-back opportunities to test course structure and organization and provide foundational data to apply for curriculum development, not just for our course, but for additional team-taught courses through the National Science Foundation. In 2005 we submitted a CCLI (course curriculum laboratory improvement) grant to NSF, and were funded in 2006 for Grant Award 0536681, "Increasing Scientific Literacy for Non-Science Majors Through Team-Taught Interdisciplinary Lab-Based Courses." The grant established a commitment to further team course development and substantial assessment.

The specific objectives of our grant were to:

- Alleviate science anxiety.
- Enhance students' awareness of the principles of scientific inquiry, thereby creating a base of knowledge about how scientists ask and answer questions. Our objective was for students to understand that science is one of several ways of knowing and to recognize both the power and the limitations of the scientific approach.
- Increase multidisciplinary learning by modeling how different disciplines approach related scientific problems with different techniques and perspectives through team teaching.

- Increase active learning by the development of laboratory-based components to familiarize students with scientific methodology and aid in the development of critical thinking skills.

Based on the first course offerings with our team, we developed an overall structure to be applied to all team-taught courses. Each course shares three common features: first, to consider the study of science as a way of knowing; second, each course will be team taught from two disciplines; and, third, each course will incorporate laboratory-based experiments.

The study of science as a way of knowing includes discussions on modes of inquiry. Students should understand that science is one of several ways of knowing and recognize both the power and the limitations of the scientific approach. Students should understand the definitions of science and appreciate that scientists use testable approaches through predictive hypotheses that generate interpretable data. The second shared theme focuses on multidisciplinary, team-taught approaches to science. From this perspective, students will see how different fields address common questions, using a variety of techniques that support the validity of scientific tenets. This interconnectedness, often underappreciated by nonscientists, is in large part what gives scientists confidence that their understanding is correct. In addition, each course will be based in active learning and hands-on laboratory experiments where students will practice the scientific method. Courses will be capped at 48 students per course (24 students per lab multiplied by 2) to allow individual attention from faculty.

With these goals in mind, and two course offerings already completed, we began to look at the evolution of our team-taught course on evolution.

THE DEVELOPMENT AND EVOLUTION OF ORIGINS: SPECIFIC GROUPED PEDAGOGIES

Building an Integrated Class

Our initial approach to designing the course focused, probably too much, on showing the differences between our two disciplines and outlooks. Team teaching is unusual for students, and we wanted to make sure that they understood the advantages and unique aspects of learning from multiple perspectives. We also wanted to justify the value of team teaching, since our course was serving as the pilot for a new sophomore-level "Doing Science" course in Otterbein's core curriculum. Another factor was our perception that students and the general public often naively lump all science together. In fact, it is not uncommon for our colleagues in other disciplines to refer to a "science" department, while no one would accidentally lump psychology, sociology, and political science into a single "social science" department.

What we began to realize as we taught the course, however, was that focusing too much on the differences tended to lead students to dichotomize the material, which actually hindered them from engaging in active integration and synthesis. The other issue was that when the students perceived the course as two entities marching side by side, they became concerned with logistical and structural issues that tend to get in the way of learning. They want to know which approach is "right," which answer should go to which instructor, and, most important, which approach they should know for the test. In response, as we refined the course over multiple offerings, we worked to make the course more cohesive to help students connect with and integrate the two viewpoints.

Course structures

"Origins" meets twice a week (one hour and 45 minutes) for 10 weeks, and course meetings are divided into three formats: lectures, laboratory exercises, and structured discussion meetings. Only 10 of the meetings are dedicated to lecture, six are used for laboratories, three for discussions, and one for a midterm exam. As science professors, we were originally concerned by the lack of "information" content that we could include in the course, since science courses typically have lab sessions that augment, rather than replace, lecture time. It was also initially difficult to decide who got to include which favorite topics, since the 10 lectures were divided between us, and the first lectures were on science and science methodologies, not the "origin" topics per se that we were most interested in. Predictably, the first offerings of the course were packed with too much, so we have had to let go of several good topics. For example, an original goal was to give students examples of how evolution affects their lives today through topics such as the evolution of antibiotic resistance in pathogens. Amy's lecture on pathogen evolution ("Dr. Darwin") was a favorite with students, but ultimately it was integrated into the class in different ways to slow the pace of the course and allow enough time to handle the core concepts.

Lectures

A single lecture for an hour and three-quarters would far exceed normal student attention spans; therefore, we always include a five-minute break after the first hour. Dividing the class period into two sessions could allow us each to teach for half the period, but in practice we seldom do that. Initially we tried to do this, but invariably the second lecture was short-changed and became rushed. Even when the first lecturer was diligent in staying on schedule, tardy students, course announcements, handing back papers, and students lingering at break all led to less time for the latter lecture. In addition, for the first few weeks of the quarter, we give short quizzes that we feel are necessary to force the students to keep up and to practice our testing style, but the quizzes almost always took more time than we wished. We addressed this problem by changing to quizzes on the course management system that must be completed online prior to class time. Other reasons for not splitting lecture periods between the two faculty include a longer treatment of the topic, more coherence within the day, and the ability to plan and revise until the last moment without the need to consult with the other faculty member.

Despite a single person being "in charge" for a day, the other still attends and is part of the course in several ways. First, lectures invariably start and end with "business" announcements that we do jointly. Second, many of the lectures are designed to include short contributions from the second person. For example, although Amy generally lectures on science methodologies, the lecture calls for examples on testing hypotheses, and at this point we each give examples from our disciplines. Amy describes a classic example of experimental science in cell biology, while Hal discusses an example of hypothesis testing in historical science—the hypothesis that an asteroid triggered the extinction of the dinosaurs. In a later lecture on the self-correcting nature of science, Amy describes how the paradigm of passive diffusion through cell membranes that was taught for many years has now been replaced by the idea that membranes hold many specialized channels through which different sorts of materials move. Hal discusses the case of Piltdown man and how the fossil went from being regarded as an important human ancestor to being revealed as an infamous hoax. Having the second faculty member insert a short example or module within the other person's lectures seems to be a good compromise that fosters integration, while at the same time allows for coherence within the class period.

Integration between faculty comes from successive paired lectures that provide different approaches to the same topic. For example, in our discussion of evolution, Hal generally presents the Darwinian view of evolution, discussing natural selection as the principal mechanism for the evolution of new organisms. This lecture is paired with Amy discussing how evolution proceeds on the molecular level. Molecular mechanisms for evolution include DNA mutation, rearrangement, and the newly appreciated role of changes in the rates and timing of development (the so-called evolutionary toolkit). Thus students are presented with the process of evolution from the viewpoint of the organism, for example, as preserved in the fossil record, and then from the viewpoint of the DNA, as investigated by molecular biologists.

A second example occurs when we address the origin of humanness. Hal begins the conversation by discussing the fossil record of hominids and how associated artifacts (tools, art) reveal the evolution of human intelligence and creativity. Students are asked to define the moment when hominids become "human" based on their artifacts. Amy follows this lecture with a discussion of the differences between humans and apes based on DNA, brain structure, and genes for language. She also includes the molecular basis for how our brains have developed the capacity for creativity and consciousness.

Lab exercises

A critical goal in designing our course was the incorporation of lab activities, so that students could model doing science. The activities needed to be short enough to complete in a limited time (an hour and a quarter), and the labs needed to be paired so that a paleontological lab was offered at the same time as a molecular biology lab. During the first day of lab, half the students would complete one lab and half the other, with students switching the second day. The methodologies, and the types of specimens used in the two disciplines, are very different, so it was a challenge to design labs that were both relevant to a given part of the course and in some sense complementary.

Again, our path over several offerings of the course has been to make the labs more similar and better integrated. For the first offering we each designed our labs independently and only had a vague idea of what the other person intended to have the students do. Luckily, during the first offering, enrollment was limited to no more than 24 so that all students completed the lab together, and so that we, as instructors, could attend and complete each other's labs. This helped us improve each other's labs since we were experiencing them from a student's point of view—that is, we were largely out of our comfort zone. More important, this first offering was the only time we got to experience the other labs, so it has been crucial in our ability to field student questions about the labs, and in allowing us to draw interconnections between the labs.

Our pattern of refinement for each of the three pairs of labs was the same. For example, our first pair of labs during the initial course offering were the "Origin of Cells Lab Exercise" and the "History of Life Lab," and they were numbered on the syllabus as labs one and two. Later labs were numbered three through six. We each designed and wrote the labs without conferring in detail with the other. In our minds the two formed a logical match. In the cell lab, students used microscopes to examine living bacteria that represent the first and simplest life forms. They also examined nucleated cells and identified cellular organelles, which, as we had discussed in class, evolved at a later date from the permanent incorporation of symbiotic bacteria. They also looked at the similarity of different nucleated cells from the diversity of modern phyla.

In the paleontological lab, students examined the rock record of the early life forms, similar to the living examples studied in the cell lab. Bacterial fossils, and evidence for the rise of atmospheric oxygen (from bacterial photosynthesis), first occurred over three billion years ago and were followed more than a billion years later by the larger and more complex nucleated cells. Fossils of multicellular animals from the late Precambrian and Cambrian were also examined in the lab to document the rise and diversification of all the modern phyla. To us the two labs represented the two halves necessary to recreate the initial evolution of life: the modern living organisms and their physical evidence in the past.

Students did not make the connection so easily, however. During the first offering, students completed the cell lab first (subsequent students were allowed to complete either lab first), and Hal was amazed during the paleontology lab how little connection the students saw with the cell lab. It seems that in the cell lab they learned about cover slips and focusing microscopes and sketching blobs, while in the paleontology lab they tried to remember the order and ages and eras and names for various fossil creatures. Despite having observed and sketched non-nucleated and nucleated cells, students could not come up with criteria to distinguish between the two groups in the fossil record where the nuclei are not preserved (non-nucleated bacterial cells are smaller and simpler in outline).

For the second iteration, we decided to incorporate a sheet of questions that explicitly required students to integrate and synthesize material from the two labs. The students still got a lab handout in the cell lab and one in the paleontology lab, but they also got an additional sheet of paper with the synthesis questions. For example, one question asked students to connect fossil representatives from the paleontology lab to the stations in the cell lab that examined bacteria and nucleated cells. Another asked students to describe the geological evidence that Miller and Urey were correct in performing their experiments in the absence of free oxygen, even though oxygen is abundant in the atmosphere today (in lab, students saw rocks with minerals deposited before the atmosphere was oxygenated).

The synthetic question sheet may have helped, but we agreed that the students were still viewing the two labs as disparate and were failing to make the desired connections. In response, in subsequent offerings we merged the two labs into parts A and B of a single lab, "The Early History of Life and Complexity of Form: Geological, Cellular, and Developmental Perspectives." There is now only one lab handout but it contains three parts: the Cell Lab, the Paleontology Lab, and the synthetic questions. Students submit a single lab for grading, though as instructors we still each grade the questions pertaining to our labs, and a share of the synthesis questions.

Our other two pairs of labs have followed a similar trajectory: they began as related yet independent labs, and we subsequently merged them into two halves of a lab with a single name. Our "Evolutionary Process" lab has a "Genes" part and an "Organisms" part. In this case, the genetics of evolution is modeled using various kinds of beans (a lab modified from Benz, 2000), while natural selection at the organism level is modeled using jelly beans of various colors (prey items) and giving students spoons of different sizes (bird beak sizes). The two labs are similar enough to be viewed as a natural pair (both use types of "beans," both look at changes over a series of iterations, and both create data that are graphed and analyzed), while at the same time demonstrating distinct principles. The importance of dominant and recessive alleles and how DNA changes are modeled in the genes part, and the concepts of fitness and adaptation are modeled in the natural selection part.

Our final lab, the "skull lab," has students reconstruct human evolution through the use of life-size skull models. Originally, only one of the labs used skulls, following a modified version of the "skull lab" developed by Craig Nelson and others (Nelson, 2001; Nickels, n.d.). In that lab students compared human and ape skulls and a series of Hominid fossil skulls, thus graphing the change through time in various characters from ape-like to human-like. The second lab focused on the developmental evidence for human evolution using developmental models of various organisms and microscope slides. Once funds became available, we rewrote the latter lab and purchased a series of model human and chimp skulls of various ages (fetal–adult). Students now examine how skull shape changes as humans age and discover that prior to birth human head shape is nearly indistinguishable from that of chimps. The relatively larger brains and flatter faces of adult humans arise because their human growth trajectories do not slow as rapidly during development as they do in chimps (neotony). The current lab, therefore, has two parts that deal with very different aspects of evolution, but both use similar types of evidence (skulls).

Structured discussion

Incorporating discussion into science courses is often tricky, since the issues scientists engage in are so dependent on evidence, and students' grasp of evidence is often limited. Yet in structuring the course, we both knew that more active teaching techniques can aid student learning, and that many students in nonscience disciplines expected "discussion." We also reasoned that discussion would give both instructors a chance to weigh in at the same time, and show that scientists do have individual viewpoints. Therefore, we have incorporated three "jigsaw" discussions into our course. In our jigsaw exercises, each student is assigned one of four readings to complete prior to class. Students must bring a typed copy of their answers to questions on the readings as their "entrance ticket" to the discussion for the day. In class they group with peers who completed similar readings, and they all spend the first half of class discussing the questions and becoming experts in the topic. For the second half of the period, students reassemble into groups containing one expert in each of the four readings. Students then teach their colleagues about their material, and learn the material in the other three readings from their colleagues. Ultimately, the groups are given a synthetic exercise that requires them to draw on the information from all four readings, and the students discuss possible solutions before writing up their answer (generally a one-page, single-spaced essay) outside of class.

The jigsaws have proven very successful in the class. During class time we both move about informally, stopping and discussing the material with the various groups and frequently heading off to a group with a raised hand. There are generally eight or more groups consisting of two or three students for each of the readings. The two of us work through the room independently, discussing the material with the students and often answering somewhat related class questions. Since each of us visits each group once or twice, the students hear our individual views, but not in a setting that can be construed as confrontational. A common complaint that we hear from students about team teaching (in other classes) is that the two instructors bicker back and forth about the right answers. Our approach minimizes this divisive, if often inaccurate, perception.

As we used jigsaw discussions, we began to realize that they actually functioned to "trick" students into extracting and manipulating data toward larger scientific questions. Students were reaching scientific conclusions without the usual accoutrements (and in some cases phobias) of doing science. For example, our first jigsaw, modeled on one by Craig Nelson (2001), assigns students to read behavioral accounts of one of four apes (chimp, bonobo, gorilla, and orangutan). Students read excerpts from a variety of sources and look for examples of behaviors such as caring, kissing, tool use, and self-awareness. Ultimately, the students use the information on the four species to place the traits on a biological tree to determine the evolutionary origin of traits they had assumed were unique to humans. Similarly, later jigsaws have students reflect on the imperfections of the human body (readings from Morgan, 2000, on the evolutionary origins of bad backs, acne, obesity, and lack of fur), and the evolutionary origins of human behaviors (readings from Diamond, 1992) on animal examples and evolutionary origins of art, promiscuity, doing drugs, and growing old. For the synthesis assignments, the students write one-page essays on whether, on balance, the human body appears to be a "well-designed" machine, and how their personal behaviors are affected by their evolutionary roots. These topics are close to the students' lives and engage them, while at the same time teaching some very important lessons, such as that the human body has many quirks left from its evolutionary development, and that even behaviors and creativity have evolutionary roots.

Assessment of students

While subject matter and pedagogy are most important to educators, unfortunately the bottom line for most students is assessment. Nothing quells the students' interest in learning like angst over testing. We try to make it very explicit in our testing what we expect of each person, who will be writing questions on which subjects, and who will be grading them. We originally gave individual review sheets before our exams, but we now give a single handout that has separate parts (for example, lists of vocabulary) for the different instructors' contributions. We also each write questions on our own material, though in practice we both carefully read and edit all questions. Students therefore know that the questions will be fair, and that their essay answers will be graded by the person who taught the specific material. Grading is facilitated by grouping questions on the exam page so each of us can grade specific pages before handing the exams on to the other instructor.

It is also useful that we met and agreed early on to a general theme of our testing. While different styles of testing stress either recall or concepts, we have agreed that the type of question we like to ask is for the evidence behind a particular scientific conclusion, rather than recall of the conclusion itself. We tell the students this up-front. We also promise the students "synthetic" questions that ask them to draw together different parts of the course and, often, material presented by the different instructors.

With five iterations of the course and continual refinement, we are optimistic that we've found the right balance of integration at different levels in the class. We've balanced the proportion of lecture to lab activities to class discussions. We've balanced the contribution of each member of the team within these areas of the course, and we've blended and integrated the topics to create a consistent voice. The question that remained was how successful we really were at connecting with the students and how well the students were meeting the outcomes we had designed for the courses.

Assessment of courses: Measures of success

How did we actually measure the success of the course? Certainly built-in assessments—the labs, the exams, and the papers written by students—are the major markers, and we designed the assessments with the outcomes in mind. It's always a good idea to measure what you actually hope they'll learn and practice. Evidence from the courses on these assessments suggests that many if not most of our students are meeting the content outcomes we outlined.

But how do you actually measure successful team teaching? In many ways it's intangible. It's recognized anecdotally by each team member and differently from year to year. The challenges of every course vary, as faculty who teach individually or as teams will attest. The makeup of the student body in each course, the commitments to other projects, research, campus service that each member of the team experiences all make every course offering its own unique opportunity and challenge. However, we have made significant efforts to assess, both qualitatively and quantitatively, when appropriate, the impact of team teaching in our classroom over time.

Using both pre- and posttests before and during our NSF-funded curriculum development, we looked at the impact of our course and that of other team-taught courses on students' understanding of science methodology, science anxiety, and course-to-course comparison longitudinally of individual teams, with students reporting on team-teaching experiences.

From 2004 to the present we assessed nearly 200 students in the team-taught courses and compared this to nearly 150 students who took the more traditional junior- and senior-level courses. We had students from every department on campus reporting from over 40 majors in our pool of surveys.

Three sections of "Origins" were included in the surveys as were two sections of a team-taught course, called "Atoms," taught by faculty in physics and chemistry, as well as two sections of "Why Sex" taught from a molecular and physiological perspective by faculty in life sciences.

If we focus first on general attitudes toward team teaching, we find that students who participated in the team-taught classes overwhelmingly reported a positive experience. However, teasing apart team-teaching successes is more difficult due to the diversity in the teams and the specific topic of each class.

If we look specifically at the longitudinal impact over the three Origins courses offered during the survey period, we see a significant positive trend of reported positive experiences in the course.

We were also interested in the impact of these courses on reducing reported science anxiety. Of all the students surveyed for all science courses, 48% reported some level of anxiety associated with the course on the pre-survey. Within this group of students, after analysis of the demographic information, anxiety on the pre-test positively correlated with their previous high school experience, with the correlation significantly higher in women than in men, in alignment with previous surveys by Tobias (1985) showing gender to be a significant predictor for science and math anxiety. However when levels of anxiety in women compared with those in men were examined more closely, anxiety was high regardless of previous high school experience.

As a result of the pre-survey findings, we were particularly interested to see whether the team-taught courses taught earlier in the curriculum would have an impact on self-reported anxiety. Unfortunately, when the 200-level team-taught courses were compared to the standard 300- and 400-level courses, neither course was shown to make significant improvements in reducing science anxiety for women or men, independent of the grade the students received.

Therefore, it was somewhat surprising, given the tenacity of science anxiety that persisted in the courses, that there was a significant impact on students' perception of the value of science in society as a result of the courses. They report overwhelmingly on the importance of learning to be scientifically literate regardless of gender, major, year in college, high school experience, GPA, or anxiety levels, which was consistent in all courses, including team-taught.

Equally surprising was the fact that all students reported on the importance of lab activities in learning, with no statistical significance between courses that formally included hands–on, lab-based activities (team-taught courses) and those that did not (upper-level lecture courses).

But even though all students reported equally on the importance of hands-on, lab-based learning, we were able to show that those who participated in the team-taught courses could identify and define scientific methodology at a statistically significant ($p = 0.001$) higher level than could students in the upper-level lecture courses, showing that actual practice of scientific method does correlate with increased understanding.

Variables that probably influenced this effect are:

- lab-based activities where they practice the scientific method;
- smaller classes where they have more interaction with faculty; and
- team-taught interdisciplinary topics that stress the use of method to answer similar questions from different disciplines.

Therefore, with the assessments suggesting that team teaching was making a difference in students' understanding of science as a way of knowing and the value of science in society, we can reflect on the overall experiences with this project.

REFLECTIONS AND LESSONS LEARNED

Reflections From Amy Jessen-Marshall

Every team's experience with team teaching will be different because the personalities of the individuals and the combination of personalities will always be unique. I have had a variety of team-teaching experiences, but only some of them have been formalized and extended throughout the entire course. This chapter on the Origins course with Hal represents my most extensive and repeatable experience. But I have also taught with other faculty for other extended full-length courses, as well as in shorter versions, mini-courses, presentations, and informal facilitation of student groups. In some cases my experiences share common themes worth noting and commenting on. In some cases the experiences are anecdotal stories, unique experiences no one else should necessarily expect to encounter, but valuable because they have shaped my expectations and my skills of navigating the team-teaching experience.

A consistent theme I find in team teaching and student response is the challenge of gender difference on the team. Both courses I have formally taught as a member of a team have been me, a woman, paired with a male colleague. The outcome of this situation can manifest itself in a variety of ways. My experience is that students tend to assign gender roles when given the opportunity in ways that they don't when I teach alone as a female instructor. In numerous examples from both teams in which I have participated, students, both male and female, automatically assume that when they need help, or need to ask for an extension or explain a problem, they should come to me, that I will be the more tolerant, open, or perhaps the "easier" faculty member with whom they can speak. The types of arguments presented to me when I play a role in a mixed-gender team are different from the types of arguments presented to me as a member of a same-gender group or as a solo instructor.

I had one young male student refer to Hal and me as a "married couple," commenting on the communication style that he seemed to observe between Hal and me as equivalent to the way his mom and dad negotiated their relationship in public. I wanted to ask him if I was playing the role of mom or the role of dad, but I didn't because his interpretation was obvious.

The role of mom is a challenging one to navigate when as a solo instructor I never find myself having to adopt or more specifically resist that role. When I am a solo instructor, the majority of students seem to see me as gender neutral; I am simply a scientist, a microbiologist, or a cell biologist depending on the class, who happens to be a female. I don't encounter the same emotive behavior that students, in particular male students, seem to attribute to me when I teach with my male colleagues. Interactions when I am a solo instructor involve more direct questions focusing on content, deadlines, or methodology in labs, but rarely complaints related to level of difficulty, challenges to expectations for deadlines, or requests for support with writing and interpretations of data. This situation is similar with female students, but in my experience to a lesser degree. When I compare this situation to my experiences facilitating learning groups with other female faculty, I see little of this behavior in students.

As a result of our experience with gender differences and team teaching, my colleague, Hal, and I have had focused discussions about the specific roles we play with students. We found that students' increased emphasis on perceived gender roles had the potential to create a rift between the two of us as teachers, as students attempted, consciously or not, to place us in conflicting positions. To prevent this, we agreed that it was important, when dealing with many student issues, that I take the harder stance with students, that is, bad cop, while allowing my male colleague to play the more supportive role—good cop.

For example, we faced situations with student plagiarism on several lab reports, where one student had taken language from a partner's report. When discussing the consequences with the students, I began with the more stern rebuke, allowing Hal to follow with confirmation of how we needed to handle the situation. In this way, the students saw a united front and a consistent message. While it has been difficult in some cases, it has forced us to take clear positions, and it has been important both for the students and for us as a team to model that, as a team, we set the standard for the class. It hasn't completely prevented the students from trying to manipulate us differently, but it has reduced the discontinuity that I believe some students felt the first several times we taught together, and it has relieved the potential for conflict between my partner and me.

I would argue that as a follow-up, this need to stand united has actually raised the rigor of the courses as we hold not only the students but each other to a high standard. I truly believe I've become a better teacher for having taught repeatedly with Hal. When we began teaching Origins together, it was a subject that was peripheral to the subjects I had previously taught at Otterbein. The principles of evolutionary theory are foundational to my disciplinary research and the questions I ask, and interpretations of experiments only make sense with an evolutionary framework, but I had never taught evolutionary theory for its own sake. As a result, when we taught the course together for the first time and, I would argue, the second, third, fourth, and fifth times, I was learning from Hal, right along with the students. I constantly reinterpreted and made new connections between the evolutionary evidence available from the fields of geology and paleontology, which Hal teaches, and the fields of microbiology, cell, molecular, and developmental biology, where I am more comfortable and have more expertise. One outcome is that I blend the topics together now, referring to examples from Hal's areas to reinforce my own.

A second outcome is that I am more critical of my own teaching. When Hal and I teach together, we attend every class we can, listening to each other, adding comments during class, and sometimes challenging each other. Having another expert in the room keeps me on my toes. I probably spend twice as much time preparing my lectures because I know if I leave a hole, or misrepresent something because I've hurried, he'll be there to question me and make me rethink and rephrase the details more carefully. At first, this was incredibly intimidating, but now I've come to appreciate it. Teaching with Hal means I'm more reflective about all of my teaching. I'm always thinking about the gaps and worrying through the transitions, aware that my students can't make the connections if I can't make them myself.

I suspect Hal's experience may be somewhat different. His research is steeped deeply in questions of evolution, and he had more experience teaching the topics than I did before we began. He invited me to be a part of this course, and he had a clear vision for it. I brought a perspective from different fields, but my guess is that my contribution was not quite as eye-opening for Hal, but it more likely reinforced the foundational understanding he already brought to the course. However, one area that has grown in the course is the discussion of evolution and developmental biology, drawing on books by Sean Carroll (2005, 2006), which are written for the general public. Carroll uses the metaphor of the toolbox to explain how a small subset of genes can be used to explain large-scale body plans and developmental organization. I distinctly remember a conversation Hal and I had as we were preparing to teach the course for the second time. I was using the chalkboard in his office to explain splicing and alternative gene regulation and how the gene toolbox made sense in light of the total number of genes in our genome, and the apparent disconnect in the number of proteins in the cell based on recent updates on the human genome project. I suddenly realized that I did have areas of expertise that could challenge the expert, which is what I consider Hal to be when we teach evolution together.

Over the years I have also become an expert, and as the course evolved, so did our comfort with each other's topics. The reality of academic schedules and conferences, and life with children, meant that on occasion we called on each other to step up to teach a topic we normally covered. In the years we've taught together, I think we have now covered nearly every lecture. I have taught the foundational ideas of Darwin and natural selection, and the perceived conflict between religion and science, while Hal has stepped in to teach the developmental biology and questions on the origins of consciousness.

Looking back through the evolution of our course on evolution, we can see shifts in emphasis, adjustments in topics and schedules. The development of the syllabi is telling, and Hal outlined this earlier in the chapter. What is harder to see, but I believe is just as real, is the evolution of our partnership. The electricity in the classroom is still there, the challenge of a constant collegial expert doesn't go away, at least not for me, but the recognition that my partner in the classroom will prod me always to bring my best to the classroom is a positive energy, only realized because of the shared experience we've had working through the challenges of content, organization, student concerns, and feedback.

I think it is also important to compare this to my other team-teaching experience. I have taught with another colleague outside of my department, and we have offered two iterations of the course, so I have some context in which to reflect on the more limited but similar evolution of the course. In this case I would say the results have been more mixed. When I reflect on the differences in the experiences, I find different teaching partners draw on different parts of my personality. While I consider myself to be more of an introvert than an extrovert, teaching with Hal forces me to draw on the energy required to be extroverted in the classroom. My other team-teaching partner shares more of my introverted traits, which has made it more challenging to maintain my energy and easier to slide into a quieter form of teaching that doesn't draw the students in nearly as much. As a result we've had more challenge connecting to the students, the topics continue to be more disjointed and not yet as well integrated, and I find myself working harder to sort out ways to shift our pedagogies to more class-led discussions that we can both facilitate.

I think it is too soon to predict what will work with this team-teaching partnership. But what it has taught me is that expecting the same experience with every person you teach with is delusional. I have discovered the communication patterns, the pacing, the cues that reinforce good teaching are varied, and each partnership requires a different level of investment.

Agreeing to teach as a member of a team should come with the self-reflection of what your individual strengths are and, equally important, what you perceive as your weaknesses. Will your team member complement and buoy your strengths, allowing you to grow and feel challenged in the classroom? Or will the partnership reinforce your weaknesses and make the classroom experience a struggle? Understanding roles and responsibilities is key. Team teaching isn't for everyone and should never be forced. I've seen assigned teams end in catastrophe. But a good partnership can result in a classroom with experiences that are more than just the sum of the expertise of the teachers. It can become an experience on its own, unique to the personalities of the teachers and students involved, with connections that one would never make as a solo teacher.

Team teaching requires a certain vulnerability. I've found that I have to be both vulnerable and confident to make it work. I have to be open to compromise with and critique my partner, and yet be confident enough to stand on my own and take the best of the critique forward to influence my teaching. Writing this reflection echoes this. Hal and I have had these conversations, and we've reinforced the experience in the classroom, but putting it on paper creates a different level of vulnerability. As I end, I am left wondering at his reaction. Only time will tell as we continue to teach together where we will end up by the time we have taught the 10th course together.

Reflections From Hal Lescinsky

As Amy suggested, any pair of instructors that engages in true team teaching will develop a relationship that will be on display in the classroom. Students, in turn, will often interpret the relationship using the stereotypical patterns with which they are most familiar, such as husband/wife, good cop/bad cop, or boss/underling. The relationship will also be exploited by astute students who desire leniency or extra help, so it is imperative to examine and monitor the relationship since it becomes, after all (and perhaps regrettably), an integral part of the students' classroom experience.

The development of the good cop/bad cop and husband/wife divisions along gender lines, as happened to us, is probably typical, and I have seen it lead to almost comical results. For example, in a previous team-teaching experience, I co-taught with a young female colleague who was not married and did not have children. Part of the course was a travel experience, and we found ourselves overseas having to "hand-hold" immature students, and all too often help them with the most basic of life skills. With children of my own, I was accustomed to this and not particularly bothered, while my colleague was quite irritated. Yet she was the one they generally approached first with trivial questions.

While students may focus on the personal minutia and love to watch for squabbling between faculty pairs, it is the academic relationship that develops during teaching that is particularly stimulating and valuable to us as faculty members and, we hope, to the students as well, at least in the long run. Even with years of teaching in a classroom, having a peer sitting in the room with you makes the experience different. There is a real vulnerability that makes me strive to ensure that my information is up to date and correct in every detail. An additional concern that was even greater for me in this team-teaching experience was to make sure my teaching style and pedagogy were flawless. Amy had won the school's "Young Teacher of the Year Award" for her excellence in teaching just a few years earlier. Would I be a flop in her eyes as a teacher? Ultimately surviving the shared vulnerabilities led to a strong camaraderie between us and a shared sense of accomplishment in the course.

Vulnerability issues are particularly intense when it comes to student evaluations. In our case, during the first couple of offerings we handed out two sets of evaluations on the same day, almost forcing a comparison between the two instructors and certainly dividing the course into "his and her" parts in the students' minds. Several weeks later, when we received our individual results, we would talk about the general trends but without show-ing the absolute numerical data. The effect of separate evaluations, at least to me, was divisive and negated the principle that the course was an integrated whole in which we played different yet complementary roles.

Later on, since we were both tenured, we chose to give out a single set of evaluation forms. This was an important decision because it meant that now we were both responsible and vested in the class. It was not sufficient to do our individual part and then wash our hands of the other person's contribution. The course in its entirety was important, and our annual review materials would now depend, in part, on our teammate. In my mind, it was at this point that we were fully invested and that the course became the fully integrated whole that I think is ideal.

Another positive aspect of the team-teaching "relationship" was devel-oping a scholarly colleague. At many small schools, each faculty member's charge is to cover a particular academic arena. Departmental faculty are col-leagues in a social sense, but they may have little interaction in their scholarly pursuits. The team-teaching experience meant that both of us were pursuing the bigger picture of evolution together, including topics such as human consciousness and the evolution of language in which neither of us had any real expertise. As a result, we were both on the lookout for new cases and examples, and we began to regularly trade links, articles, and book reviews as they came out. We would share interpretation of and amazement at new findings in a scholarly way that was directly relevant to each of us. With our different backgrounds and insights, we helped each other put the advance-ments into perspective. For example, Amy was able to relate advances in our understanding of *FOX* genes (a key to language), and I could shed light and a fossil perspective on the discovery of hobbit man (*H. floresiensis*).

In summary, team teaching can be a benefit not just to the students, but to the faculty as well. Although there are certain relationship issues and vulnerabilities to work through, if these are negotiated successfully, the expe-rience can be very rewarding. The team-teaching experience can build deep professional and intellectual bonds with a colleague that are very different from the typical intrafaculty bonds. When both team members are fully ves-ted in the course's success, they are learning together and practicing the best aspects of integrated learning.

REFERENCES

Benz, R. (2000). *Ecology and evolution: Island of change.* Arlington, VA: National Science Teachers Association Press.

Bower, B. (2001). Math fears subtract from memory, learning. *Science News, 159*(26), 405.

Carroll, S. (2005). *Endless forms most beautiful: The new science of evo devo.* New York: W. W. Norton.

Carroll, S. (2006). *The making of the fittest: DNA and the ultimate forensic record of evolution.* New York: W. W. Norton.

Cross, K. P., & Steadman, M. H. (1996). *Classroom research: Implementing the scholarship of teaching.* San Francisco: Jossey-Bass.

Diamond, J. (1992). *The third chimpanzee: The evolution and future of the human animal.* New York: HarperCollins.

Haynes, C. (2002). *Innovations in interdisciplinary teaching.* American Council on Education/Oryx Press Series on Higher Education. Westport, CT: Oryx.

Michael, J. (2002). Misconceptions—what students think they know. *Advances in Physiology Education, 26*(1), 5–6.

Modell, H., Michael, J., & Wenderoth, M. P. (2005). Helping the learner to learn: The role of uncovering misconceptions. *American Biology Teacher, 67*(1), 20–26.

Morgan, E. (2000). *The scars of evolution: What our bodies tell us about human origins.* London, UK: Souvenir Press.

Nelson, C. (2001, April). Creation, evolution or both? A multiple model approach. *Chautauqua Short Course for College Teachers.* Dayton, OH: University of Dayton.

Nickels, M. (n.d.) *Hominid cranium comparison.* Retrieved from http://www.indiana.edu/~ensiweb/lessons/hom.cran.html

Tobias, S. (1985). Math anxiety and physics: Some thoughts on learning "difficult" subjects. *Physics Today, 38*(6), 60–68.

Tobias, S. (1990). They're not dumb. They're different: A new "Tier of Talent" for science. *Change, 22*(4) 11–30.

2

Lessons Learned by a Philosopher and a Biologist in Team Teaching a First-Year Seminar on "Disease and Culture: Why You Are a Walking Petri Dish"

Min-Ken Liao and Sarah Worth

THE PLANNING

The First-Year Seminar (FYS) Course at Furman University

Furman University's pedagogical model of "engaged learning" offers students opportunities to develop skills in problem solving, critical thinking, and experience-based education. Simultaneously, this model challenges professors to develop courses and research programs that strive to meet the goals of "engaged learning." In spring 2006, with this mission in mind, the faculty voted to change the structure of the traditional general education requirements (GER) program that artificially compartmentalizes the experiences of a liberal arts education into departmental offerings only. The faculty agreed that the new GER requirements are meant to facilitate "students' understanding of the transferability of intellectual processes and knowledge across contexts whose complexity may supersede the boundaries of individual departments or disciplines" and to bring "a greater variety of intellectual perspectives into meaningful dialogue with one another, thus highlighting for students both the complementarity and the uniqueness of departmental and disciplinary voices" (*Invigorating*, pp. 6–7). The goal of this new program is "to foster the capacity to integrate knowledge across disciplines while still respecting disciplinary expertise and authority." The objectives of Furman's new distribution requirements encourage faculty members from different disciplines to develop interdisciplinary courses. With this new initiative we decided to embrace this fully and develop an interdisciplinary course involving an intersection of biology and philosophy.

Furman University began to require first-year students to participate in a First-Year Seminars (FYS) program in fall 2008. The ultimate goal of the FYS program is "to introduce students to the intellectual life of the liberal arts college." Students and faculty members in the seminar should strive to foster qualities and skills such as enthusiasm for learning and reflection, critical consideration of established knowledge, critical evaluation of preconceptions and assumptions, and appreciation of the research process. Although the goal is undoubtedly admirable, it is challenging to reach these objectives in one course taught by one faculty member trained in one discipline. Therefore, we, a microbiologist (Liao) and a philosopher (Worth), proposed to develop and teach an interdisciplinary course called "Disease and Culture: Why You Are a Walking Petri Dish." The preliminary objectives of this interdisciplinary course were (1) to use the study of infectious diseases to arouse students' curiosity and interest in the scientific bases and cultural, historical, and societal impacts of diseases; (2) to enhance students' understanding and appreciation of the research process; and (3) to use established scientific knowledge as background to evaluate preconceptions and assumptions critically and ethically.

We believe that, through the collaborative effort of two faculty members with distinctly different disciplinary backgrounds, our course development will result in course content and teaching approaches that would broaden and enhance students' learning experience by extending their ability to appreciate various disciplinary perspectives. This interdisciplinary team-teaching approach will underscore the importance of learning varied perspectives on a topic and will expose students to an interdisciplinary way of learning. We believe this type of collaborative and interdisciplinary interaction in and of itself is a powerful demonstration to students that focused, interdisciplinary, team approaches to the pursuit of knowledge are at the core of a liberal arts education.

Interdisciplinary Opportunities Mini-Grant of Associated Colleges of the South (ACS)

We believe that the best way to teach interdisciplinary courses is to *demonstrate* the interdisciplinary way of learning to our students. Therefore, we started by teaching each other our own disciplinary techniques. Liao attended an entire semester of Worth's Introduction to Philosophy (Liao had unfounded fear of philosophy because she dropped a philosophy course in college and took logics instead), and Worth spent two and a half weeks in Liao's research lab learning microbiology/molecular biology techniques and helping to pre-run the kits we planned to use for the course. We engaged in extended dialogues throughout the year prior to the actual course. We immersed each other in our own disciplines by learning firsthand the kinds of activities we planned to do in the course, which helped us to design our lesson plans and avoid potential pitfalls. Additionally, we read/viewed numerous books and films and identified several that were appropriate for the class. Together we developed lesson plans, activities, and materials that guided the course. We anticipated that the course would be challenging, yet intellectually stimulating for the students.

We also received an interdisciplinary opportunities mini-grant from Associated Colleges of the South (ACS), which provided the financial support necessary to prepare us to function fully as a team in teaching this course. The grant covered our two-and-a-half-week stipends for developing (Liao) and testing (Worth) laboratory activities during the summer. It also allowed us to purchase potential books and media for the course. Finally, the grant paid for post-class conference travel so we could share our ideas with others.

The Nature of the Course

In addition to lectures and discussion, our FYS course had a laboratory component because we believe that engaging, hands-on experiences enhance learning. This course was also writing-intensive because we believe that writing is an important exercise to process and distill information and to foster insights. Based on Worth's two-and-a-half-week research experience in the biology lab, a set of laboratory exercises were developed and modified for first-year college students. (Worth's biology skills were probably significantly lower than what an incoming freshman's skills might be at Furman since she had not darkened the door of a biology lab since the eighth grade.) We also participated in a First-Year Seminar Writing workshop that helped to prepare faculty members who were interested in teaching writing-intensive FYS courses. Table 2.1 portrays the basic lecture schedule provided in the syllabus. We had 12 students, the maximum number for an FYS-Writing course. Each week, we met for six hours—three for lectures and three for laboratory exercise/movies/discussions.

We anticipated that our students would be challenged by the course content that spans dual disciplines and by the classroom discussions and writing assignments that demanded them to assess established knowledge critically. Additionally, we hoped this course not only would change our students' perspective on the topic, but due to the intensive and frequent

Table 2.1   Schedule

Tentative Lecture Schedule

Date	Topics	Reading	Writing	Lab
Week 1	Introduction Lecture and discussion		First writing assignment: 2-page narrative on your experience of an illness	Lab: Taking notes Film and discussion: *Typhoid Mary* Writing: What is good writing?
Week 2	Labor Day Holiday Lecture and discussion		Identify a disease for writing and presentation	Lab: Bacteria in the environment Writing: Peer review
Week 3	Library tour Film: *Rx for Survival #1* *The Ghost Map:*	Chap. 3	*Start research on the historical aspect of the disease (part I)*	*Lab: Getting information from biological journals/books* *Discussion: Rx for Survival #1*
Week 4	Discussion: Cholera and *The Ghost Map*	Chap. 3	Research and writing; the historical aspect of the disease (part I)	Lab: Epidemiology Lab: PBS *Typhoid Mary's* interactive game Writing: Find a partner Film and discussion: *Rx for Survival #2*

Week	Topic	Chapter	Assignment	Activity
Week 5	Discussion: Cholera and *The Ghost Map*	Chap. 3	Turn in Part I Start research on the social aspect of the disease (part II)	Movie: *Erin Brockovich*
Week 6	Test #1 Lecture: TB Fall Break	Chap. 7	Research and writing; the social aspect of the disease (part II)	Field trip: Wastewater treatment plant
Week 7	Discussion: TB Film: *Rx for Survival #3* Discussion: TB	Chap. 7	Turn in Part II Start research on the scientific aspect of the disease (Part III)	Lab: Microbes and health Discussion: *Rx for Survival #3* Film: *Rx for Survival #3*
Week 8	Lecture: Plague Discussion: Plague	Chap. 5	Research and writing; the scientific aspect of the disease (Part III)	Lab: Oral bacteria Lab: Microbes and health (cont.)
Week 9	Lecture: AIDS Film: *Rx for Survival #4* Discussion: AIDS	Chap. 5 Chap. 11	Turn in Part III Working on putting all parts together and add conclusion	Discussion: *Rx for Survival #4*
Week 10	Discussion: AIDS	Chap. 11	Working on putting all parts together and add conclusion Return part III with comments	Speaker

Table 2.1 (Continued)

Tentative Lecture Schedule

Date	Topics	Reading	Writing	Lab
Week 11	TEST #2 Lecture: Syphilis Discussion: Syphilis	Chap. 6	Working on putting all parts together and add conclusion	Movie: *Philadelphia*
Week 12	Discussion: Syphilis Film: *Rx for Survival #5* Discussion: Syphilis	Chap. 6	Turn in the first draft of the full paper Start working on presentations	Lab: Microbial controls Discussion: *Rx for Survival #5*
Week 13	Lecture: Malaria Film: *Rx for Survival #6* Discussion: Malaria	Chap. 8	Working on presentations	Lab: Gel electrophoresis Discussion: *Rx for Survival #6*
Week 14	Discussion: Malaria Student presentations	Chap. 8		No lab this week
Week 15	Assessment/Focus group interview FINAL EXAM			

* Readings from Sherman, I. W. (2007). *Twelve diseases that changed our world.* Washington, DC: ASM Press.

interactions that we would have, it would inevitably change the way we teach our own courses and conduct our own scholarly activities in the future.

TEACHING

Classroom Activities

We chose eight diseases (ulcer, typhoid, cholera, tuberculosis, plague, HIV, syphilis, and malaria) about which students had to learn biological and epidemiological concepts and history, and to understand some of the relevant social/cultural issues that either currently or historically attended each disease. Although lectures are not the only way to convey information, it is a format with which most first-year college students are most familiar. Therefore, numerous mini-lectures were scheduled to lay the foundation of information needed to understand each disease. We did not spend the same amount of time on each disease, and we did not cover every aspect of each disease. Rather, we used each disease to demonstrate different biological and cultural aspects. As shown in Table 2.2, students did learn quite a few key concepts in biology, particularly in microbiology and epidemiology. We did not introduce these concepts to students in the manner and order that most biology textbooks do, however. Rather, we associated different concepts with different diseases to make the information more applicable. We also deliberately chose current issues that were relevant to the students' lives to better foster classroom discussions. For example, we began the course talking about the salmonella outbreak that had happened the previous summer, getting students to think about the risks and benefits of recalling food (widespread fear and financial breakdown for the tomato growers) versus letting possibly infectious food get into the market (human suffering and death). Because this was also a writing-intensive course, we lectured on writing and common logical mistakes in writing and dedicated several portions of our laboratory time to peer review and learning to edit.

We assigned three books for this course. One of the assigned texts was a grammar handbook. We also assigned *Twelve Diseases That Changed Our World* by Irwin W. Sherman for background information on various diseases, and *The Ghost Map* by Steven Johnson. We chose a set of films that also played an important role in the class. We watched PBS's *Rx for Survival, A Global Health Challenge* (six-film set) and followed each episode with lively discussions. We also watched *Erin Brockovich, Philadelphia,* and *Miss Evers' Boys* to demonstrate some of the complex social issues attending a disease that we could not convey in a lecture.

Table 2.2   Discussions

Use this disease	and this . . .	to teach . . .	and to discuss . . .
Ulcer		Koch's postulates	Scientific methods and animal models The ethics of animal testing and animal rights
Typhoid	NOVA: *Typhoid Mary, The Most Dangerous Woman in America*	Introduction to epidemiology Introduction to microorganisms Introduction to infectious diseases	How to discuss with civility Quarantine and civil rights
Cholera	Book: *The Ghost Map* by Steven Johnson Field trip: Wastewater treatment plant Film: *Erin Brockovich*	Cholera Introduction to evolution Introduction to bacterial genetics: transformation, transduction, and conjugations Introduction to GIS Introduction to water treatment system	Compare and contrast privilege and entitlement: Is clean water a privilege or an entitlement? What constitutes privilege? What constitutes entitlement? When privilege becomes entitlement and when entitlement becomes privilege
Tuberculosis	Take flu shot together as a group	Introduction to immunology Introduction to tuberculosis Introduction to vaccines	Illegal immigrants and public health (pathogens know no boundaries) Social justice Privilege and entitlement revisit Moral obligation of vaccination
Plague	*Impact of the Black Death on European Culture and Church Authority* by John Doyle	Introduction to plague Introduction to disease cycle Introduction to ecology: prey and predator	Religions and culture: Jewish history and Black Death Does Bible shape our views on diseases?

Use this disease	and this . . .	to teach . . .	and to discuss . . .
HIV	Film: *Philadelphia*	Introduction to viruses Introduction to central dogma of molecular biology Introduction to HIV and AIDS	AIDS and Botswana (case study): *Closing the Gap: Antiretroviral Therapy for the Developing World* by Robin Pals-Rylaarsdam Change of social and cultural perceptions: Is it better now? If so, why and how?
Syphilis	Film: *Miss Evers' Boys*	Introduction to syphilis Introduction to Nuremberg trials and Belmont report	Ethics in research Informed consent and IRB: too little or too much
Malaria	Fundraising for mosquito nets	Introduction to eukaryotic microbes Introduction to malaria Introduction to population genetics: malaria and sickle cell anemia Introduction to eugenics	Do we have moral obligation to others whom we don't know and won't meet? What is humanity? Is eugenics gone? Artificial reproduction technology

To enrich our students' learning experiences further, we invited three outside speakers: Dr. Beverly Connelly, director of the infectious disease program at Cincinnati Children's Hospital Medical Center, to talk about childhood vaccination; Dr. Sandra McLellan, associate scientist at the Great Lakes WATER Institute, to talk about wastewater contamination in the freshwater; and Mike Winiski, associate director of the Center for Teaching and Learning at Furman University, to lecture, demonstrate, and provide students with hands-on experience with GIS (geographic information system). All three speakers were able to give insights into aspects of epidemiology that we would not have had the expertise to do. This was another example, we think, of the importance of multiperspective information.

Writing

We assigned the students six writing assignments. The first one was a two-page narrative on each student's own experience of an illness. This was intended merely as a diagnostic writing assignment for us to make a preliminary assessment of our students' writing ability. In the end it turned out to be a very interesting icebreaker for the class as well, as students ended up sharing very personal information about themselves and their history with illness. For instance, some had never dealt with anything more severe than the common cold, while others had dealt with infected bug bites leading to severe cellulitis and severe digestive problems while living as a missionary in sub-Saharan Africa. As it turned out, students' history dealing with their own illnesses had a great impact on how they viewed others' suffering from (and possible responsibility for) the diseases we learned about.

Starting the second week, each student found a partner, and each team of two selected one disease (not taught as a subject in class) as the subject of their writing assignments and an oral presentation. Although each pair could search collaboratively and share information about the selected disease, each student had to turn in individual writing assignments. Five writing assignments after the diagnostic writing followed: three assignments on three aspects of the disease—the historical, social, and scientific aspects; the first draft of the compiled (three previous parts integrated) paper; and the final paper.

Worth gave two lectures related to writing: one on using logos, pathos, and ethos in writing, and one on logical fallacies commonly made in writing. We also invited a librarian to talk about information literacy. We both read and graded every writing assignment, so each student received two sets of comments (in different ink colors) and the average of two grades for each writing assignment. In addition, we encouraged each pair of students to review each other's writing, and we met together with every student for a writing conference after the first draft of the full paper.

Student presentations

In addition to writing a paper, each pair of students gave an oral presentation to the class. We decided to have oral presentations for two primary reasons. First, we would like to use as many ways as possible to assess students' learning, so in addition to writing assignments and written tests, we included oral presentation. Second, a student's ability to convey information verbally uses a significantly different skill set from either writing or written tests. For their presentations, we encouraged students to present the information creatively. All students used PowerPoint to present the information and skits, games, snacks, and video clips to further engage their audience. The experience of preparing for the presentations was probably more memorable for the students than was the presentation itself.

Lab exercises and field trips

In addition to meeting three hours a week for lectures, this class met one afternoon a week in a three-hour block for laboratory exercises, films, extended discussions, and field trips. The laboratory exercises exposed students to basic microbiology laboratory skills, such as aseptic technique, streak and spread plates, staining, use of microscope, ELISA (enzyme-linked immunosorbent assay), and gel electrophoresis to illustrate basic concepts such as Koch's postulates, epidemiology, antimicrobial activities, and immunology-based assays.

We also had two field trips: one was a visit to Western Carolina Regional Sewer Authority (WCRSA) Pelham Wastewater Treatment Plant in Greer, South Carolina, to see exactly how wastewater is handled while we were reading and discussing *The Ghost Map* (a fascinating social history of the invention of epidemiology, how cholera was identified as a waterborne disease, and how it all started with just one dirty diaper getting into the water supply). Students were more engaged than we had expected during the wastewater treatment plant visit; almost everyone asked questions. Our other field trip was to the university's infirmary to get flu shots while we were lecturing on and discussing the science of vaccination, herd immunity, and the moral aspects of vaccination (although some students still refused the flu shot, alas, citing anecdotal evidence for the treatment's ineffectiveness).

Assessment of Students and Teachers

We used tests, writing assignments, and oral presentations to assess how well students mastered the content of the course as well as the disease they chose to write about (Table 2.3). To assess whether remaining course objectives were met, we used a SurveyMonkey questionnaire and a focus group interview. Figure 2.1 includes the questions. The bold questions were sent to students before the focus group interview via SurveyMonkey. The Survey-Monkey questionnaire, due before the focus group interview, served two purposes: (1) to shorten the time needed for focus group interviews, and (2) to present a framework for the assessment to avoid digressions during focus group interviews.

The conversation in the focus group interview was taped and transcribed. Students' biggest concern was the writing assignment—not just the research and writing parts, but the grading part as well. Their major worry

Table 2.3 Assessments

Assessment	Method
Content	3 tests/300 points
Laboratory activities	Quizzes/50 points
Writing	6 assignments/500 points
Oral presentation	1 presentation/100 points
Participation	50 points
Course evaluation	SurveyMonkey and focus group interview by Winiski and Boyd

was that their writing had to please both of us. To them, our differences (race, culture, disciplines, teaching styles, likes/dislikes, and more) represented potential opposing views, and they were unsure how to please us both. We were then more able to address directly the notion that both of us would recognize good writing, despite our differences.

REFLECTIONS ON THE COURSE

We anticipated that this course would demand the time and energy of a full course for both of us, and the administrators agreed. The actual workload of a team-taught course was about what we expected. We also expected that, based on the title of our course, most of our students would be interested in majoring in science or in careers in allied health. This expectation turned out to be incorrect. Our students had very diverse academic and career interests; their intended majors were health and exercise science, environmental science, communication studies, art history, biology, biochemistry, sociology, and Spanish.

We expected our students' writing ability to be basically adequate, and we were right. There were not many grammatical or structural errors in their writing, and most of them knew how to research and organize information and put it in writing. What they needed to work on were engaging introductions, better transitions between sentences and paragraphs, making theses more visible, and staying focused. All of their final papers improved significantly from their first drafts.

What we did not anticipate was that having two instructors grading the students' writing would cause such major anxiety for them. One of the things we inadvertently did that may have caused their anxiety was to discuss in

Figure 2.1 Questionnaire

OVERALL PERCEPTION

Briefly describe your FYW. Assume we don't know anything about what you've been doing and perceived goals of the course.
How could the experience be improved?

CONTENT

What three mini-lectures stand out in your mind? Why?

Here is a list of the diseases you have learned: cholera, GIS, TB, plague, AIDS, syphilis, and malaria.

Here is a list of the mini-lectures: Central dogma and HIV, epidemiology, GIS, evolution, immunology and TB, Koch's postulates, plague, rabbits and viruses: what do microbes want, syphilis, the Belmont Report and the Nuremberg Code, and malaria, human genetics and eugenics.

We have discussed a few social/cultural issues. Can you name one that stands out in your mind? Here is a list of issues: cholera and clean water, TB and illegal immigrants, AIDS relief in Botswana, syphilis and human subjects, malaria and moral obligation of global health, eugenics, and vaccination.

What three issues/topics stand out in your mind? Please provide specific examples of why they stand out.

WRITING

What was one new thing you learned this semester about the writing process?

What was one new thing you learned this semester to improve your writing?

Describe your writing process.

One goal of the FYW program is to help students value writing as a way of thinking. Was that your experience? Why? Why not?

Has what you learned about the rhetorical triangle changed how you approach learning? Writing?

Has your writing assignment helped you learn?

VIDEOS AND FILMS

The first video we watched was about Typhoid Mary. What do you like the most about this film? What don't you like?

What impressed you the most about Rx. for Survival? The content, cinematography, stories, scripts, or narrator?

Numerous issues were explored in Rx. for Survival. Which issue impressed you the most?

We watched three movies: Erin Brockovich, Philadelphia, and Miss Evers' Boys. Are they good choices? Are they thought-provoking? Should we use them again?

Are these videos and films effective in facilitating discussions? Which is (are) "must use again"? Which is (are) "watch it if you have time"?

Figure 2.1 (Continued)

LABORATORY EXERCISES

You are receiving NW (Natural World) credit for this course. Do you think the lab exercises are too much, too little, or just right for the NW credits?

Here is a list of labs you have experienced this semester: bacteria in the environment, getting information from biological journals/books, epidemiology: finding patient zero, field trip, microscopic examination of oral bacteria, which mouthwash works for me, what makes yogurt, AIDS diagnosis, microbial controls: chemicals and spices, and gel electrophoresis.

SPEAKERS

We had two speakers: Dr. Beverly Connelly from Cincinnati, Ohio, and Dr. Sandra McLellan from Milwaukee, Wisconsin. Both of them are extremely distinguished in their respective fields. It took their time, our time, and our money to have outside speakers. **Do you think their seminars enhanced your FYW experience? Should we invite outside speakers again?**

GROUP DYNAMICS

List three ways your classmates affected the learning environment.

What impact has working in groups had on your learning? How is working in groups going (context: discussion, peer review, outside of class)?

How worthwhile was it that we went to the wastewater treatment plant?

How was the balance of class discussion between professors and students? Did everyone have a chance to participate? What could the professors do differently in the future to improve class discussion?

How was the experience different from courses you had in high school?

MIX OF ACTIVITIES/USE OF CLASS TIME

We have exposed you to a lot of activities. Now try to look back on them and identify which activities, assignments, and resources have had the biggest positive impact on your learning. Be specific about what helped.

Which activities, resources, or assignments were the least helpful to your learning?

What specific ideas do you have for improving the least helpful activities, resources, or assignments?

We had a number of things going on simultaneously in our course: library instruction, writing instruction, speakers, videos, writing assignments, mini-lectures, class discussion and group presentation. Was it a cohesive experience? Why or why not?

HANDLING CHALLENGES

Please describe any experience where you felt as if you were in totally new territory.

What aspects of the class were especially frustrating or overwhelming? Please explain.

What were your expectations for the course? How demanding is the work compared to your expectations?

Figure 2.1   (Continued)

REFLECTING ON LEARNING / CONNECTIONS

Can you give me an example of a time you thought about a _____ *[topic] outside of class? When? Where? What did you think about? In what way?*

Did your worldview change as a result of the class? How? Give a specific example.

How has your idea of infectious diseases changed as a result of this experience?

Did you have a "Eureka!" moment during the class? Please tell the story of that moment.

How will this experience support your learning in other classes as you continue your education at Furman?

Has your perception of scientists and the work they do changed as a result of this experience? How?

How would you rate your effort and dedication to learning the course material?

The freshman seminars are intended to be "incendiary"—to light intellectual fires. Did this course get you "fired up" about the subject matter or the chance to express your own original ideas in writing? If yes, how and when? If no, what could the professors do to ignite your intellectual passion?

ASSESSMENT

Have the graded assignments provided a fair opportunity for you to demonstrate what you have been learning? Please explain. If you feel there's a gap, please suggest specific ideas that would help.

---

front of the class whether they should use passive voice in their writing. As a philosopher, Worth fought against passive voice, and as a biologist, Liao argued for it. We should have decided in advance of the class, but literally showing the students that we had different standards raised their anxiety about their written assignments. They spent a great portion of the focus group interview talking about this. While we thought that averaging our individual grades on their writing would reduce the impact of our personal preferences, students did not see it this way. They believed they had two sets of standards to follow and two professors to please and that it would be impossible to please both of us simultaneously. It was interesting to note that the grades each of us gave for each assignment were almost always identical.

What we also did not expect was that students seemed to pay more attention to *how* we communicated than *what* we communicated during many of our discussions. Since our professional training (and cultural background) is so different, we often argued from different perspectives and emphasized different things. We expected students to notice and appreciate our "different ways of knowing." We thought this was one of the *benefits* of an interdisciplinary course (the whole point is that we have different perspectives), but it really caused anxiety in a few students. As indicated in the Furman University Student's Response Form, the anxiety was mainly about not having correct, final answers to some issues. Additionally, we did not realize that our facial expressions, body language, and emotions during discussions were also of great interest to students. The evaluations indicated that this was significant for them, and their comments about it were pleasantly positive. As some students pointed out, we demonstrated how to present different opinions with respect and humor, and how to reach consensus. As educators, we knew that we influence students; we just did not realize the degree of influence until the course.

We had a $250 budget for each FYS course for social activities, such as meals or movies, to encourage "class bonding." We convinced our students to donate the money to buy insecticide-treated mosquito nets for people in sub-Saharan Africa where malaria is a major public health concern. Our students even took an extra step. For the bonding experience that was supposed to be paid for with the funding, the class decided to bake cookies together (to bond) and then held a bake sale (to raise money for more nets). All of the cookie money went to buy mosquito nets, an outcome that was beyond our expectations.

When we teach this course again in spring 2011, we will make two major changes: We will (1) incorporate genetic diseases and (2) ask our students to generate writing rubrics. Because Liao is a microbiologist, we felt more secure dealing with infectious diseases the first time we taught the class, and we realized that public health would be an important topic of discussion. However, we did not expect public health issues to dominate the majority of the discussions. While these issues are relevant, important, and interesting, we would like to expand the scope of discussions. Thus, we plan to incorporate genetic diseases such as Down's syndrome, schizophrenia, Huntington's disease, Rett syndrome, fragile X syndrome, and Duchenne muscular dystrophy. These diseases cannot be cured, and some do not even have effective treatments. We think they will make students think about issues such as resource allocation and fetal rights. In addition, we plan to include some intentional discussion of writing rubrics. We did not provide rubrics before because we did not think we needed them. We gave comprehensive oral instructions in class and detailed comments on each assignment, sent students electronic messages regarding their writings, discussed writing in class, met with them individually for writing, and provided a grammar handout. Yet, students were still very anxious about how they were graded. Therefore, next time we will devote a class period to generating a rubric by asking students themselves to identify the important categories in a piece of writing and to describe what qualifies as inadequate, adequate, very good, and exemplary in writing. We hope this new approach, in addition to the ones we took last time, will provide better guidance and ease students' anxiety about writing.

REFERENCE

Invigorating intellectual life: A proposal for Furman University's academic program and calendar. (2005, September 10). Report to the Furman Faculty from the Curriculum Review Committee.

3

Arts and Community

Lessons in Team Teaching

Robert A. Richter and Margaret E. Thomas

Connecticut College is currently implementing a variety of cross-disciplinary approaches in the curriculum, one of which is team teaching. As we all know, team teaching is expensive, and faculty are often encouraged to find other, more cost-efficient ways to collaborate. But sometimes special opportunities for team teaching, like ours, come along. It's a story worth telling, filled with lessons learned. We'll begin by placing our team-teaching experience in context and introducing the unique opportunity that brought together a director of arts programming and a music theorist.

GETTING STARTED

In 2006 Connecticut College received a three-year grant from the Sherman Fairchild Foundation that enabled the college to offer three new collaborative courses per year. Each year the courses included a first-year seminar, an intermediate-level course, and an advanced course. The grant stipulated that the courses be cross-disciplinary within the arts and be team taught by two members of the faculty from different arts departments. Remarkably, the grant provided funds for both faculty members to be replaced for one full course in their home departments so the regular curriculum in the respective departments would suffer no negative impact. The grant also provided each course with a significant budget to support visiting artists, field trips, class activities, and equipment. This wonderful project gave the college, arts departments, and faculty an opportunity to collaborate with their colleagues in new ways, and it provided our students with rich, arts-centered experiences.

We were both members of the steering committee that oversaw implementation of the grant program, and Margaret was the project director during the second and third years of the three-year grant. Margaret is an

55

associate professor of music who specializes in music theory. Robert holds a
staff position as director of arts programming in which he oversees the college's performing arts series and some artist residency programs. While we
both had an interest in participating in the program directly, neither of us
had potential course proposals or teaching partners in mind at the outset.
There were a number of reasons why we were drawn together to develop and
teach our course. First, the initial set of proposals submitted by faculty was
lacking in first-year seminars, a type of course in which Margaret was interested. There was not an obvious colleague for her to collaborate with, however. Robert expressed an interest in teaching, which he had never done
before. We were friendly acquaintances at the time, and we both sensed that
we would work well together; fortunately, this proved to be true! We decided
to pool our interests to develop a new team-taught course. Our first challenge
was to find subject matter for our collaboration that used our strengths and
expertise; the next challenge was to figure out how to bring our disparate
experience to course design and implementation.

Throughout his career Robert has been involved in the arts in a number
of ways, as an actor and director, a teaching artist, an administrator, and a
presenter of the performing arts. He has a bachelor's degree in anthropology
and theater and a master's degree in liberal studies. Early in his career he
made his living as an actor and a teaching artist, teaching programs in a wide
range of settings, including schools, community centers, and even correc-
tional institutions. Before coming to Connecticut College, he worked in history museums, where he specialized in using the performing arts, primarily
theater and music, to interpret the museum's collection. Part of his work at
Connecticut College is to oversee the college's performing arts series, under
whose aegis professional artists or companies are brought to campus to perform and present some form of residency activity either on campus or in the
community. Those residency activities range from a simple master class for
college students to a music workshop for preschool students to creating a
film with middle school students. Robert also has conducted significant
research on Eugene O'Neill, which resulted in a book and numerous essays
on the playwright. Robert's education, interests, and work experience have
always crossed disciplinary lines.

Margaret, on the other hand, brought to the project a traditional set of
disciplinary skills. Her bachelor's degree is in violin performance, and her
graduate degrees are in music theory. Her teaching had always focused singularly on music theory, at a range of levels to be sure, but safely within the
confines of the compositional and analytical techniques of tonal and post-
tonal western music, along with related ear training. Probably her greatest

initial contribution to the collaboration was the experience of some 15 years' worth of college teaching, which led to skills in course design, classroom management, and course website design, along with an understanding of the college's academic climate.

Given our disparate backgrounds we settled on a course called "Arts and Community," which would explore the different ways the arts and communities intersect, support each other, and create each other. Robert had expertise in the area, along with important ties to the local community; we were both interested in the topic; and it was ripe with potential as a course for first-semester college freshmen. So our extensive planning began. Right away we established regular, weekly meeting times, which we carried out for a full six months leading up to teaching the course; this provided a critical forum for getting to know each other better, sharing readings, developing ideas, revising drafts of the syllabus, and the like. In the end, what emerged was an ambitious course plan with five main organizational challenges: (1) it was a first-year seminar, which, per college policy, meant that it included 16 freshmen, was a "writing-enhanced" course (requiring a substantive amount of graded writing), and it required Margaret (as a full-time faculty member) to serve as academic adviser for all 16 students; (2) it was to be team taught and emphasize arts collaboration; (3) it would be funded through the arts collaboration grant, which provided for guest artists and course supplies; (4) it was to be a service-learning course, a feature suggested by the course topic and one that required development of "community partners" (sites at which our students could perform their weekly service learning), a service-learning assignment for each student relevant to his or her background and interests, and monitoring the service-learning activities of the students; and (5) our course would meet one evening a week for three hours—a result of Robert's status as staff rather than faculty—which made it vital that we use a variety of techniques during each class to keep students engaged not only during a single class meeting (employing experiential, collaborative activities in addition to traditional lectures and discussions), but also during the long gap between our class sessions, which could prove to be particularly problematic for freshmen.

Clearly, in addition to normal course preparation—writing the syllabus, developing reading and writing assignments, developing the course website, deciding on modes of assessment, and the like—our "Arts and Community" course required choosing and scheduling guest artists, developing the service-learning component, and, most especially, determining how to manage the team teaching itself. It was important to both of us that it be true team teaching, and not some kind of "tag-team" teaching; we were to do the work together, both in and out of the classroom. The first order of business was to continue our regular weekly meetings even after the class was underway. This assured us of time to plan each course meeting in detail and consult on student progress and grading; in hindsight it reveals how deeply our team teaching informed every aspect of the course.

SYLLABUS AND COURSE DESIGN

Each of the five challenge points listed previously necessitated careful planning. Our basic course description for the syllabus sought to give a glimpse into the course's special nature for the students. To schedule all of our special events and guest artists, plan our budget, and develop relationships with service-learning partners, we had to develop a very detailed plan for the semester well before it was underway. Once we determined that the course would focus on arts and community, we both undertook a kind of professional development, since the topic was tangential to both of our areas of expertise. As a result, we worked independently to become better acquainted with the issues and find potential readings. We then shared our findings with each other, eventually building a set of weekly topics and settling on textbooks and other readings that would support them well. By the time the syllabus was completed and the course had begun, we were able to include a specific set of topics and reading assignments, along with listing roughly half of the guest artists. The syllabus, shown in abbreviated form in Figure 3.1, reflects this planning.

We also gave careful thought to modes of teaching and assessment. As we developed the course we decided early on that this would not be a test-based course; we wanted the concept of community, which was so critical to the course topic, to infuse the learning experience. To that end we designed assignments, papers, and projects that could be shared among class members through discussion and collaboration. We decided that lecturing had no place in this course, and that we would favor class discussion and experiential learning during class sessions. This was due in part, of course, to the fact that this was a seminar class with 16 students, which automatically suggests discussion-based teaching, but also to the subject matter. As we worked out the details for each week, however, the specific topics suggested differing approaches to each meeting that carried a unique balance of classroom activities.

A Typical Week

The success of team teaching hinges on strong communication between the faculty, being a single voice for the students, and developing a rhythm with

Figure 3.1   Syllabus

FYS 172: ARTS AND COMMUNITY
CONNECTICUT COLLEGE

Fall 2007
Meeting time: Thursday evenings, 7:00 p.m.-10:00 p.m., in Blaustein 205

Team taught by:

Rob Richter, Arts Programming	Midge Thomas, Music Department
Palmer Auditorium, room 304A	Cummings Art Center, room 223
ext. 5069	ext. 2728
raric@conncoll.edu	metho@conncoll.edu

Course Description:

This course will include: (1) an examination of the concepts of "community" and "arts"; (2) an introduction to the concept of community arts, through a study of formally presented arts, participatory and community-based arts, and arts as an essential element of education and community enrichment; (3) exposure to the local community, through service-learning projects, attending performances, visiting museums and galleries, and interacting with arts professionals (guest artists and lecturers); (4) active collaboration, with each other, the instructors, and the community.

This course is supported by the Sherman-Fairchild Grant, which allows funding for visiting artists. This will allow us to enrich the course with visits from a range of artists, including Sara Juli, and representatives from the Aquila Theatre Company and the Liz Lerman Dance Exchange.

You can access the course web page via the college's website: go to either the library or academics page, and then to the listing of course web pages. It is a ConnCourse site, for which you will need a user id and password in order to login: your id and password should be the same as those you use to log into the college's server. The website includes the course calendar and assignments, links to readings and other pertinent websites, information about your grades, the class discussion board, and more.

If you have a physical or mental disability, either hidden or visible, which may require classroom, test-taking, or other reasonable modifications, please see one of us as soon as possible. If you have not already done so, please be sure to register with Susan L. Duques, Ph.D., in the Office of Student Disability Services, at Extension 5428.

Course Materials:

Two books are required for purchase, and are available at the college bookstore: *Cultural Democracy: The Arts, Community, and the Public Purpose*, by James Bau

Graves; and *Performing Arts Presenting*, by Kenneth J. Foster. Other materials will be on reserve in Greer Music Library (in Cummings Art Center). We will also be reading articles from the "Community Arts Network" website (http://www.com munityarts.net/readingroom).

Coursework and Grading:

Coursework will include:

- weekly readings or other assignments
- service-learning activities (2–4 hours per week)
- a journal documenting your service-learning and artistic experiences
  - a journal topic or question will be posted as an assignment on the course website by Friday, 5:00 p.m., each week, and your response must be submitted online by Monday, 5:00 p.m., each week
- attendance at the three events listed on the course schedule, along with *three additional* events chosen from the list given below (other events might be possible, with our approval)
  - a one-page report on each of the three additional events is due within one week of the event
- two short papers of 2–4 pages each
- a final project that will emerge from your service-learning work.

Grades will be calculated as follows:

35%   Preparation, participation, and attendance (including attendance at class, artistic events, and your service-learning site; evidence of preparation for class; and your performance at your service-learning site, the evaluation of which will be based on feedback from the site supervisor)

20%   Journal

20%   Short papers and event reports

25%   Final project

Attendance Policy:

Because we meet only once per week (13 meetings in all), your attendance is crucial! Absences will be excused only under extreme circumstances. Unexcused absences will impact your class participation grade. In addition to our regular meetings, as a group we will attend the OnStage performance of Sara Juli on Oct. 18 (during regular class time), the OnStage performance of the Aquila Theater on Fri., Oct. 26, and a portion of the Books, Brushes, Jazz, and Blues Festival in downtown New London on Sat., Sept. 8. Reliability and attendance at your service-learning site is vital to the goals of the course, and will impact your grade, as well.

Office Hours:

We encourage you to meet with either of us with questions about the course at any time! Prof. Richter's office is located at 304A in Palmer Auditorium, and his office hours are Tuesday and Thursday, 10:00 a.m.–11:30 a.m. Prof. Thomas's office is located in Cummings 223, and her office hours are Tuesday and Thursday, 10:00

a.m.–noon. These are regular times when you can find us in our offices, and during which you may stop by at any time. We would also be happy to set up appointments at other times; simply talk to us before or after class, give us a call, or send an email. For questions related to advising you should contact Prof. Thomas.

TENTATIVE COURSE SCHEDULE

Aug. 30   **GETTING STARTED: INTRODUCTIONS**

Course overview: content, service learning
IN-CLASS SCREENING: *Open Windows*

Sept. 6   **COMMUNITY DEFINITIONS AND CULTURAL DEMOCRACY**

Service site assignments and logistics given; visit by representative of OVCS

READINGS:
- Graves, "Introduction" and chapter 1
- Foster, "Introduction" and chapter 1

Sat., Sept. 8   **BOOKS, BRUSHES, JAZZ, AND BLUES FESTIVAL IN DOWNTOWN NEW LONDON**

Sept. 13   **TRADITION AND INNOVATION IN THE ARTS**

READINGS:
- Graves, chapter 2

Sept. 20   **CASE STUDY: DANCE EXCHANGE**

Class visit from:
Peter DiMuro, Producing Artistic Director
Elizabeth Johnson, Associate Artistic Director and Teen Exchange Director

READINGS:
- Liz Lerman, "Dancing in Community: Its Roots in Arts" http://www.communityarts.net/readingroom/archivefiles/2002/09/dancing_in_comm.php
- Chris Westberg, "Liz Lerman" http://www.communityarts.net/readingroom/archivefiles/1999/12/liz_lerman.php
- Linda Frye Burnham, "Everybody Say Hallelujah: The Minneapolis, Minnesota Residency" http://www.communityarts.net/readingroom/archivefiles/2001/12/everybody_say_h_3.php

Sept. 27   **INTRODUCTION TO "COMMUNITY ARTS"**

Instructions for the first short paper will be distributed
READINGS:
- Patricia A. Shifferd, "First We Make Music: An Introduction to Music and Community Arts"

http://www.communityarts.net/readingroom/archivefiles/
2002/03/first_we_make_m.php
- Robert H. Leonard, "Grassroots, Community-based
  Theater: A View of the Field and Its Context"
  http://www.communityarts.net/readingroom/archivefiles/
  2003/12/grassroots_comm.php

Oct. 4   **THE ARTS-EDUCATION CONNECTION**

Panel discussion by education-oriented area artists

**Short paper no. 1 is due

READINGS:
- Graves, chapter 6

Oct. 11   NO CLASS: Fall Break!

Oct. 18   **PARTICIPATORY AND ACTIVIST ARTS**

OnStage Performance: Sara Juli, "The Money Conversation"
We will attend the performance together as a class, followed by
a discussion with Sara Juli.

READINGS:
- Foster, chapter 2

Oct. 25   **CASE STUDY: AQUILA THEATER COMPANY**

Class visit from member of Aquila Theater Company

Instructions for the second short paper will be distributed

READINGS:
- Graves, chapter 3
- Foster, chapter 3

Fri., Oct. 26 *** OnStage Performance: Aquila Theatre Company, *Catch-22*
8:00 p.m., Palmer Auditorium—*required event*

Nov. 1   **COMMUNITY/AMATEUR ARTS**

**Short paper no. 2 is due

Instructions for the final project will be distributed

READINGS:
- Graves, chapters 7 and 8

Nov. 8   **OUR LOCAL COMMUNITY**

**Panel discussion with representatives from local arts
organizations**

READINGS from various local media

Nov. 15   **VISUAL ARTS IN THE COMMUNITY**

READINGS:
- Tim Collins, "Lyrical Expression, Critical Engagement,
  Transformative Action: An Introduction to Art and the
  Environment"

http://www.communityarts.net/readingroom/archivefiles/
2003/06/lyrical_express.php

Nov. 29   **FORMALLY PRESENTED ARTS AND THE ROLE OF THE CURATOR**

READINGS:
- Foster, chapter 4 through the conclusion

Dec. 6   **CONCLUSIONS AND FINAL PRESENTATIONS**

the course that enabled us to work efficiently and effectively together. The best way to illustrate the flow of the course and workload for the faculty and students is to outline a typical week from one class meeting to the next. We have chosen a week in the middle of the semester as an illustration, November 1–8 (see Figure 3.1).

As mentioned previously our class met one evening a week for three hours. That evening was Thursday. Each week we had a theme or subject for the class session, which was outlined in the syllabus. This particular week the theme was "Community/Amateur Arts." The plan we developed for this meeting is outlined in Figure 3.2.

This agenda is typical of what we used for each class meeting. We both had a copy, and following it—while allowing for flexibility—helped us to stay on track. As you can see, we started the class off by discussing some of the "business" of the class and semester. We discussed upcoming course registration for the next semester, advising, and reminders about course assignments. From there we segued into activities pertaining specifically to the topic of that class meeting.

First we collected and discussed their second short paper of the semester. The assignment was to consider one of two events we had seen together as a class and discuss it "as a performance." The students were instructed to relate it to specific chapters from assigned readings. During the discussion Robert invited students to share the approach they had taken, and a broad consideration of such issues as the performative process, a performance frame, and community engagement followed. From the discussion about the papers we transitioned into a discussion about a performance of *Catch-22* by the Aquila Theatre Company that we had seen the previous week, alternating our roles as class leader. Next we focused on the online journals the students were required to write each week. It was also during this section of the class that we introduced the students to their final project/paper assignments. At this point we moved on to the core intellectual component of the day, a discussion of their reading assignment for the week.

Figure 3.2 Agenda

1. Business (5 minutes)—Margaret
   a. Are there advising or registration questions?
   b. Remind about three events, and their reports
2. Collect papers and discuss (15 minutes)—Robert
3. Discuss Aquila performance of *Catch-22* (10 minutes)—Margaret
4. Discuss latest journals and touch base on service learning (15 minutes)—Robert
5. Distribute instructions for final projects and discuss (10 minutes)—Margaret
6. Discuss reading (30 minutes)—Robert
   Chapters on "Mediation" and "Globalization and Localization"
7. Mid-semester course evaluations (10 minutes)

[break for 15 minutes]

8. Activity (60 minutes)—Margaret
   a. The performative process: turning a children's poem into a performance
   b. Divide into groups, choose poems, develop a performance
   c. Each group performs, and we discuss the experience from both a performer and audience perspective
9. Assignment for next week (5 minutes)—Robert
   a. Preview panelists/organizations—remind to be ON TIME!!!
   b. Handout

Once the discussion period was over we distributed mid-semester course evaluations, and then gave the students an opportunity to take a break. These evaluations were informal and designed to elicit concrete feedback with which we might adjust the way we conducted the remainder of the semester.

Upon returning from a short break we changed the tone of the class meeting dramatically by giving the students an experiential activity. Because the students had just completed a paper on the idea of performance, the activity emphasized the performance experience. Margaret introduced the activity—making a performance out of a children's poem—and divided the students into groups of three or four. Then each group prepared its performance; since the basis of the course was "community," Robert and Margaret routinely participated in these activities, and this evening was no exception. This portion of the class meeting culminated in the performances the students developed. We tried to have some form of experiential activity like this as part of each class to keep the students' attention during a long evening course session and to provide participants with an opportunity to put some of their thinking into practice. These activities also gave the students examples of activities they might use in their service-learning activities.

Robert closed the meeting by previewing the panel of local artists who would be visiting the class the next week, reminding the students that we would be posting online by 5:00 p.m. on Friday their journal question and giving the assignments for the week. The assignment included reading our local newspaper daily for arts coverage, and making a scrapbook of those stories, along with daily observations. The students were also to read an article on community-based arts and write three questions for the panelists for the next class meeting.

At the end of each class session, after the students left, we spent a few minutes recapping the class and determining the question for that week's journal entry. The students had to post their journal entries by 5:00 p.m. on Monday. Our choice of Monday at 5:00 p.m. was calculated. Since we met only once a week, we wanted to make sure our students had a predetermined second interaction with the class, even if it was only online. We hoped that would encourage and remind the students to keep up with their work and not leave it until just before the weekly class meeting. Monday was a good halfway point between our Thursday class meetings. For the most part this was a successful practice.

Prior to every class meeting we determined which one of us would lead a particular part of the class. We felt it was extremely important that each of us share facilitation of the class equally. This is vital to distribute the workload evenly and to ensure the students recognize us as a team. Our planning meetings occurred every Tuesday morning, which allowed us to check that the online journal assignment had been done by the night before. During our meetings we finalized the content for that week's class, looked ahead to see what advance planning needed to be done, and created an outline for the class, dividing the elements between the two of us. This particular week we had the added task of grading the papers the students had just submitted. By meeting Tuesday mornings we had adequate time to do any final preparation for that week's class.

The theme for the next class was "Our Local Community," during which we wanted to focus on amateur arts in the community. In this instance we brought in a panel of representatives from local volunteer arts organizations. The first half of the class was devoted to the guests talking about their organizations and the students asking questions, which they had prepared in advance; the second half focused on the work the students had prepared for that class (see Figure 3.3):

Figure 3.3   Agenda

---

1. Panelists representing local/amateur arts (60 minutes)—Robert will facilitate
   a. Community chorus
   b. Folk dance group
   c. Community theater group
   d. Community band

[break for 15 minutes]

2. Discussion of the panel (20 minutes)—whole group
3. Discussion of the reading on community-based arts (30 minutes)—Margaret
4. Discussion of arts coverage in local newspaper (30 minutes)—Robert
   a. Observations
   b. Scrapbooks/journals they created
5. Return papers and discuss briefly (5 minutes)—Margaret
6. Concluding business (15 minutes)
   a. Collect detailed final project proposals
   b. Distribute assignment for next week
   c. End class 10 minutes early so students can talk with us briefly individually about final project proposals

---

Once our guests had left we focused on a discussion of the week's reading assignment and how it related to our panel. From there we transitioned to a discussion about the students' observations about how our local newspaper reported on local arts events. We wrapped up the class by allowing them to ask questions about their final projects, and we returned their papers and reviewed assignments for the next week.

Assignments and Grading

We found one of the dangers of team teaching to be general confusion among the students regarding our roles as co-teachers: to whom should they turn with questions, both in and outside of class? This surely is a common problem in team teaching, one that was complicated in our case by our different statuses. As mentioned previously, we made every effort to head this off by addressing the issue of office hours in the syllabus; by confronting it explicitly during our first class meeting ("We are in daily contact with each other; you may direct questions to either one of us, and we may well consult with the other about your questions"), in the deliberate way we organized each class session, and in trying to meet with individual students together, when possible. Another critical strategy for us was to develop an approach to grading—which had implications for the design of assignments—that would enable both of us to be equally familiar with the students' work. We gave a good deal of thought to the logistics of grading as we prepared to teach the course. Not only were we planning to collect assignments each week that would require grading, but the students also were to write an online journal entry each week, which required an online response from one of us. One important concern was that we share the workload evenly; another, equally important concern was that the students were graded fairly and consistently. To address these concerns we decided that we both needed to see all student work, but that we would alternate taking primary responsibility for commenting on the work. For graded work we incorporated a consultation with one another on the grade. So, practically speaking, this meant that we alternated weeks for commenting on journal entries, and the person not dealing with journals in a given week took on the assignment that had been collected. We discussed both of these items in our own weekly meetings. We divided larger assignments (papers and the final project), each of us taking half of the class's work and making the primary set of comments on it. Then we exchanged the assignments and added a brief secondary set of comments. This way, not only were we both up to date with our students' progress, but the students knew it—as if our different handwriting weren't clue enough, we typically used pens of different colors. While this was a time-consuming process, it's important to note that we both were committed enough to the course and to our team-teaching effort that this level of work was acceptable. We did not—and even now, in retrospect, do not—see a good alternative. This approach to grading ensured that we both felt equally connected to the students, and that we were well acquainted with their strengths and weaknesses, beneficial positions when students came to one of us for help outside of class or when we read later work by the students.

THE STUDENT EXPERIENCE

All first-semester freshmen at Connecticut College are required to take a first-year seminar, enrollment in which is limited to 16 students. The college catalog states:

A sound liberal arts education should enable students to participate as quickly as possible in thought-provoking academic discussion. Freshman Seminars are intended to facilitate this process by providing students a setting for intellectual and creative engagement. These seminars introduce and support our institutional value of academic achievement through close student-faculty relationships. Seminars are designed to foster a lively and respectful interaction, both among students and between students and faculty, around a topic of the faculty member's choosing.

During the summer, before arriving at the college, incoming freshmen submit their first, second, and third choices for a first-year seminar. There are approximately 35 seminars to choose from, and the offerings encompass almost all disciplines. The students base their choices on a brief description in the course catalogue. The description for our course was:

In this course we will explore the role of the arts (particularly music, theater, dance and visual arts) in community building, including arts that are formally-presented, community-based, or intended for educational purposes. Students will participate in a variety of community projects; two to four hours of service-learning required per week.

Due to the nature of the selection process, our seminar included students with a wide range of experience and interest in the arts. For some of the students the course was their first choice, for others it was their second choice, and one student had not selected it at all. We did not learn of their level of interest until our first day of class, which presented us with somewhat of a challenge. We needed to ensure that we engaged all of our students, regardless of their interest level. We had other challenges, including the fact that the course met only once a week, on Thursday evenings, and that a large component of the course was service learning. All of the other first-year seminars met twice weekly during the day.

We found that it was vital for us to try to create a community within our own class. Many of the students were meeting for the first time, and for many it was probably the first time they had a three-hour class session and one that met at night. To create a sense of community and friendship among the students, we used the experiential activities mentioned before, which at times required students to work in pairs or small groups and enabled them to learn about each other in a nonthreatening way. For example, during our first class meeting Robert led an activity called "Common Ground," developed by the ArtsLiteracy Project at Brown University. We used a number of exercises the project developed. This activity enabled the students to see what they had in common with their fellow students and what they did not. By seeing each other's similarities and differences, students can build an understanding of each other and create a web of bonds. The ArtsLiteracy Project instructions for the exercise are listed in Figure 3.4.[1]

We adapted the exercise, and particularly the questions, to meet the needs of our class. The first question we used was "Who is an only child?" The succeeding questions built on each previous one and explored different things about the group. At the end of the exercise we took time to reflect on the activity and what students learned about each other. It proved to be a very effective community-building experience, one that we all carried through the semester.

We thought it important that if one of us was leading a particular exercise or activity, the other was actively participating with the students. We hoped this would help them to develop a rapport with each of us, which we believe was successful. The team teaching helped our students because some found it easier to identify with Margaret and others with Robert. But the students could also try to use it to their advantage by asking one of us for something, and if the student did not receive the answer he or she was hoping for, the student would go to the other. This made communication crucial between the two of us; sometimes, upon consultation with the teaching partner, we had to go back to a student and rescind a previous action or decision.

Another element of the class that was new to many of the students was the service-learning component. We required that the students conduct two to four hours of service learning each week. We had arranged for them to conduct their service-learning projects with four organizations in New London, Connecticut. They included the New London Main Street Project, which focused on revitalization of the downtown; the Dual Language Arts Academy, a bilingual magnet middle school where the arts are integrated into the curriculum; the Lyman Allyn Museum, a small art museum adjacent to our campus; and Connecticut College's Office of Volunteers for Community Service, which runs an after-school arts and crafts program at a public elementary school. The students selected one of the organizations to work with, and in most instances they custom designed their final individual project based on the needs of the organization and the student's interests. The projects ranged from developing a program to teach middle school students dance or how to play the recorder, to assisting with creation of a museum gallery audio tour to be accessed by cell phone, to design and placement of bike racks, which were also functional pieces of public art.

One goal for the course was for our students to see New London as a resource and possibly influence the students' later curricular and extracurricular activity. The service learning required that students get off campus and into the community each week and be exposed to something they normally

Figure 3.4   Instructions

COMMON GROUND

Description: Common ground can be one of the earliest performance activities used in the classroom. Students learn what they share by walking to one side of the room as a group.

Duration: 10–15 min.

Preparation: Develop and write out the list of topics described below.

Procedure: With a piece of masking tape or string or chalk, mark a line that divides the space in two. All of the students should begin together on one side of the room. Begin making statements and instruct all those who share in each trait or fact to cross the line and stand on the other side of the classroom, designated the "common ground." The list of statements should be prepared ahead of time, using the teacher's knowledge and guesswork as to the backgrounds, interests, and experiences of the particular students in the group, as well as those of young people in general. Sample topics include "Common ground for anyone who: . . . is an only child, the oldest/youngest/middle child, was born in another country, speaks a language other than English, speaks that language fluently, speaks a language other than English at home, plays a musical instrument, can sing, went to bed before 10 last night, went to bed after midnight, ate breakfast this morning, is a vegetarian, has performed in public, writes poetry, has ever won anything, can drive, can drive legally, has broken any bones, has spent more than one day in a hospital, has a pet other than a cat or dog, likes rap/country/classical music, likes to be challenged, is excited about this class . . ."

After students are comfortable, begin to insert topics related to the text(s) you might be studying in class. For instance, on a unit on Othello, topics might include anyone who has been "jealous of another person, jealous of another person romantically, jealous of another person's grades, outside of the country, in adventures in far away places . . ."

Reflection: What new things have students learned about each other? Which prompts had the greatest response? Which had the least? How did it feel to be a member of a large group in the common ground area, and how did it feel to be the only person who crossed over?

would not have had the opportunity to do or see until later in their college career, if at all.

The students were required to comment on and report about their service learning each week in their online journals, which enabled us to monitor their progress. On occasion we posed a question for the journal assignment asking the students to relate a particular class reading or discussion to their service-learning project. The journal assignments required that the students reflect on the course as a whole each week and apply what they were learning from readings and discussions.

REFLECTIONS

Robert: I felt extremely fortunate to team teach this course. I had wanted the opportunity to teach a course for some time. Margaret and I complemented each other very well. We both brought different strengths to the table, and we were both eager and willing to learn from each other. On occasion we each took responsibility for a class activity that was outside of our own comfort zone knowing that the other was there to help out if needed. In our weekly meetings we took the time to give each other suggestions and constructive criticism so that we were able to enhance our skills. As a result I know I developed new skills and learned new techniques.

A year later I had the opportunity to team teach a different course under the auspices of the same grant program. My partner in that course brought a whole different set of skills, and I found that the techniques and strategies I learned with Margaret were invaluable.

Margaret: We are extraordinarily fortunate that Connecticut College offers serious support for teaching. Its excellent Manoff Center for Teaching and Learning presents numerous workshops every semester. As we were preparing our course, we attended two timely workshops, one on service-learning courses and one on team teaching, both of which helped enormously in our course development, since these issues were new to us. One memory stands out: a senior faculty member who has team taught on numerous occasions warned us, "You had better like each other, because you are going to spend a lot of time together!" Fortunately, we did like each other, and perhaps most fundamental, teaching this course together deepened both our friendship and our professional respect for one other. Another warning from the same workshop rings true, which is that team teaching, paradoxically, is more work than teaching a course by oneself. We were initially skeptical of this warning—surely this could not be true!—but we soon discovered that, indeed, team teaching does require a tremendous amount of time, effort, and dedication. Going into a class meeting underprepared with the idea of improvising is simply not an option when a colleague is counting on you to carry your weight. Fortunately, the rewards of team teaching match the workload. We both emerged from the course with greater skills for teaching in a range of settings and with an expanded knowledge base. Perhaps most important, our students benefitted from the course in ways they would not have had just one of us taught it.

NOTE

1. The Arts Literacy Project at Brown University, "The Handbook: Building Community: Common Ground." Retrieved August 29, 2007, from http://www.artslit.org/handbook_buildingcommunity.htm

4

Interracial Team Teaching in Social Work

Mathew L. Ouellett and Edith Fraser

DESCRIPTION OF THE COURSE AND THE TEACHING TEAM

The Council on Social Work Education mandates that cultural diversity and racism be addressed as integral components of social work education. Smith College School for Social Work (SCSSW) began to act on this commitment in 1994 with a wide range of initiatives, including curriculum changes and pedagogy training to incorporate diversity content into all courses. As part of this effort, SCSSW also began to offer the course we team teach: a specific course on race and racism to represent multiple perspectives in the course. It was decided to use team teaching with interracial teams composed of one faculty member from the dominant culture and one from an ethnically diverse culture.

In the second summer of coursework (master's-level students attend three summers of academic studies with clinical placements during the intervening two years), every student is required to take the class, "Racism in the United States: Implications for Social Work Practice." This course examines the individual, institutional, and cultural manifestations of race and racism and their implications for social work clinicians. Students can choose from three different course options that SCSSW offers: (1) a class that focuses on issues from a dominant White culture perspective; (2) a "mixed perspectives" class intended to provide a dialogue space for White students and students of color to address race; and (3) a class that looks specifically at issues central for clinicians of color. All SCSSW classes convene intensively in the summer, meeting for 10 two-hour sessions over five weeks.

We first began team teaching together in the winter and summer of 1993, and we have taught together for over 10 years. Edith came to the SCSSW after teaching almost a decade at Oakwood College (a Historically Black College in Alabama). With a graduate degree in social work, Edith brought a clinical social work framework in addition to broad teaching experience. Edith's professional experience as a clinical therapist in a range of settings proved essential for addressing the unique challenges of working as a clinician of color in dominant-culture agencies and with clients from a variety of cultures. Matt came to the SCSSW after a stint with the Vermont State Department of Social and Rehabilitation Services as a child protective services social worker and then unit supervisor. At the time he began teaching with Edith, he was at the University of Massachusetts Amherst (UMA) as assistant director of the Center for Teaching. Matt's background in social justice education and multicultural organization development proved most useful in helping students understand theoretical frameworks of racism and oppression, developing tools for advocacy, and institutional and cultural change.

While we most often taught together for this period, we each also have a rich history of team teaching with others. Over this time, we have both taught with other men and women as well as with various configurations of student cohorts (that is, classes of all White students, classes of all students of color, and classes with both). Originally, we began teaching interracial cohorts of students in what we referred to as intergroup dialogue student groups. For several years, we also taught the section geared toward issues for clinicians of color. These various experiences have reinforced for us the importance of working collaboratively and using each person's strength.

Our similarities and differences enhance our in-class interaction and course development. It is important to note that we share fundamentally similar pedagogical beliefs about how to support learning about race and racism. Because of these shared values, we were able to balance structure and creative approaches to our roles and processes in the classroom. Mutual trust and respect allow us to experiment, be creative, and model what we ask of our students. It helped that we liked and respected each other as people, and appreciated each other's scholarly and teaching-related accomplishments. However, our disciplinary specialties are different enough that we each have a clear area of contribution. By acknowledging our different viewpoints and seeking them from each other in welcoming and nonjudgmental ways, we were able to talk out loud about our goals and processes as co-teachers (pedagogical, intellectual, social, and process-outcomes).

Finally, another factor in the success of our teaching team was the support of the institution, both financially and pedagogically. The school has consistently funded two instructors for each section, even in the face of budget fluctuations and competing financial demands. Additionally, every summer the program has supported a lunchtime course instructors group to bring the faculty teams together to share ideas, strategies, resources, and challenges. These lunchtime meetings became a valued time for feedback, exploring alternative pedagogical strategies, and mutual support and humor. These meetings culminated in a dinner and social gathering at the end of the term.

The advantage of an interracial teaching team is that students can observe interactions between the professors, view an authentic collaboration across racial differences, and learn how to take an antiracism position. Authenticity and transparency are essential element of these teams. Additionally, research has shown advantages of team teaching, especially in facilitating discussions on race and racism (Griffin, 1997). Such facilitation teams also offer students diverse viewpoints and model ways of grappling with complex content. As described previously, team teaching requires an extra amount of coordination, communication, and cooperation. Griffin (1997) suggests that teams also need to maintain open communication during the class, provide each other with constructive feedback, and collaboratively redesign classes and activities as the need arises (p. 93). Team teachers also need to be aware that each partner in the team will bring his or her own bias and issues related to internalized oppression (Rossenwasser, 2000) and internalized racism. On the positive side, teaching as an interracial team can lead to increased self-awareness, a greater range of strategies and pedagogical practices, and better integration of interdisciplinary perspectives into the core content. Such teams can also provide each other mentoring, feedback, and fresh perspective on student interactions.

Overview of Course Design

Because we were teaching one of multiple sections of the same course, the department drove our course description and learning outcome goals. However, we did have some latitude in how we approached the planning and implementation of the activities and assessment of students' work. We found the model of multicultural course design offered by Marchesani and Adams (1992) to be useful in helping us think through the tasks of course design. They suggest four key components to course design: teacher self-awareness and reflection, knowing our students and helping them to know each other, course content, and pedagogical strategies. Using this model, we drew from the literature and practices of clinical social work, social justice education, and multicultural organization development to arrive at an interdisciplinary approach to the core content, the learning activities, and assessment measures.

Teacher self-reflection

Central to the effectiveness of our teaching of this course was our mutual commitment to working together to plan thoroughly for the course each seminar. Doing so allowed us to respond flexibly to our students' questions, challenges, and developmental needs. We placed equal premium on process and content. To balance the process and content goals, we began each section with an emphasis on getting to know our students and building their trust in us and in each other.

We were committed to modeling the intellectual and social learning and risk taking we were asking of students. Here is an example of how this played out in our classroom. When I (Edith) had a creative idea right before or during class (usually something I thought would help students grasp a concept or technique better), rather than talk about it theoretically, I asked Matt to role-play it with me. I turned to Matt and asked if he would be willing to trust a deviation from our preplanned class.

When Edith turned to me (Matt) and asked, "Do you trust me?" I knew we were going to do something challenging and important to the concepts and practices of effective interracial group dialogue. By asking genuine questions of each other, ones that called on us to be self-reflective and to disclose our values and beliefs, we used our relationship to model a respectful interracial dialogue. We modeled trust, risk taking, and a conscious acknowledgment of our respective social power and authority. This practice underscored our key learning goal, which was the importance of developing the skills and sense of efficacy necessary to be comfortable asking questions of each other in intergroup dialogues.

Knowing our students and encouraging them to get to know each other

We value the importance of creating a learning environment where students can reflect on their prior learning, learn new information, and engage in critical discourse and analysis. We were acutely aware of the complex dynamics among ourselves, our students, our students with each of us individually, and our students with us as a team. We began by determining what we thought and felt individual students needed from each of us and from one another.

We emphasized helping students to get to know a bit about each other's social backgrounds, values, and experiences before launching into theoretical material. By building a foundation of group trust, we laid the groundwork for the mutual commitment and respect required in our future interactions to stay engaged in dialogue with each other when emotions flared. These opportunities provided a backdrop for students to understand how they had come to think and feel the way they did about race and racism. By building such interpersonal understanding first, we were able to rely on these relationships later to encourage students to listen deeply to each other, even when expressing differences.

Content

While we had clear learning outcome goals for each module of the course, we were consistently flexible in how we reached them in class. Often this meant collaborating from the very beginning on establishing learning goals and expectations collaboratively with our students. (A syllabus is included in Appendix A that details core content goals, resource materials, and learning activities associated with the course.) We began every class session with a check-in with students and would frame our discussion of the content for that class depending on what resonated for them from the readings or campus or community events.

One learning activity that exemplifies our commitment to student-centered learning and sustained dialogue is the case study exercise. Built over several weeks, this exercise began with individual reflection, moved to small-group dialogues and work groups, and ended in a collaborative class presentation. This assignment began with a brief writing exercise asking students to recall an incident from their clinical placement experiences that they thought might have had implications related to race or racism and about which they still had questions. These papers provided the basis for in-class groups of three students each. Each group picked one incident to focus on for the next steps. Students then wrote a profile (that is, a fuller description) of the incident and worked together to construct a critical analysis using the theories and models presented in class. Near the end of the term, each triad presented its case to the class.

Pedagogy

A unifying motif of our pedagogical decisions was helping students address conflicts and challenges while sustaining commitment to ongoing intergroup dialogue. Over the years, SCSSW students have often commented in their final evaluations that a key benefit of the class was the opportunity to observe two leaders from different backgrounds collaborating in a spirit of mutual respect and shared leadership, especially when the going got rough.

We regularly used a variety of group discussion designs to address the complex needs of all of our students. One such strategy we used regularly was caucus groups. These are groups formed around common social identity traits (for example, gender, sexual orientation, or racial and ethnic identities) and work well when you want to provide both intra- and intergroup learning opportunities. In the caucus group exercises, Edith met with students of color and Matt met with White students to address issues separately. Students reported that these groups allowed them a degree of comfort that is often absent in an intergroup dialogue. After the caucus group meetings, we brought the class together and each group reported to the others what they wanted their peers to know about their processes and outcomes. Caucus groups allowed us to build rapport with students, assess individual students' developmental readiness, and hear students share their experiences in a relatively supportive environment.

Caucus groups were a solution to attending to the affective learning processes of the course and often worked quite well. As experienced teachers and social justice educators, Edith and Matt anticipated and prepared for a certain degree of "push back" from students when we used caucus groups. We learned these groups could sometimes increase the tension in the room.

Such increased tension happened in one of our sections with a White female in the class whose biracial friend had suggested she register for this section with her. This White student felt she had been "invited in" as a support and confidante for her biracial friend. Thus, the White female felt misplaced in the White caucus section and became increasingly uncomfortable when the discussion dealt with White privilege and entitlement. In her discomfort, she used the whole class time to confront Matt angrily and to question his focus on privilege and power and his expertise. This exchange in itself would have been challenging, but the student included personal insults as well. The depth of her anger and the insolence of her manner toward Matt during the confrontation were wholly unexpected. This event caught us both by surprise and unprepared. Students had always quizzed both of us about our credentials, experiences, and subject knowledge, but no one had attacked us personally.

Our protocol for handling challenges until that time involved each of us taking responsibility for engaging students who mirrored our racial identities. Thus, Edith responded to confrontations or challenges coming from students of color and Matt with our White students. As this incident happened near the end of class, Matt handled it by acknowledging that the student clearly felt very deeply about her perspective and suggested that other students would have equally passionate but different perspectives. At that point, class ended and the dazed students left.

At the end of class we were shocked and confused. We each needed time to reflect before processing it together. Edith called Matt later that day and we set up a time to talk about the incident, the student, and our next steps with her and each other. When we talked later, Matt confessed to feeling shocked to the point of being speechless and Edith to being confused and unsure of what to do, given that the outburst was coming from a White woman. This led to an honest discussion and exploration of alternative modalities of intervention. What could we have done in that situation? How could we make sure neither of us felt isolated or unsupported if such a situation happened again? While Matt and the student did meet to discuss the incident outside of class, we realized later that when issues involve the entire class, they must be resolved with the entire class, too. Later, we understood that we could have called for a time-out to explore our different feelings and developed a solution as a teaching team. We could have involved the rest of the class in reflecting on what just happened (for example, a brief writing exercise or dyad discussions). Both of these were options, but they were unavailable to us in the moment due to our shock.

In the end, this incident prompted us to talk even more deeply about our formative experiences as individuals, our guiding values, and our beliefs about how students learn about race and racism. It also opened the door to our sharing more of our feelings, experiences related to our racial identities and social justice, and what we looked for in each other as teaching partners.

What Have We Learned?

Over time, we have come to some realizations about team teaching and teaching courses that challenge students emotionally and intellectually. We think these realizations may help other instructors as well.

Course design

There is no substitute for designing the entire course together. This includes establishing core learning outcome goals and core content, choosing intellectual and experiential learning activities, and designing the assessment and evaluation processes. We learned about each other's intellectual interests, experiences, and expectations for the course during these discussions. It was also in these ongoing conversations that we solidified our shared responsibility and authority in the classroom. Early on, we decided that in order to model our commitment to share authority and expertise, we would (as much as possible) co-present everything. We also made it clear to students that we made all assessment and evaluation decisions together.

Related to the planning process, we reserved time after every class to debrief. While we sometimes did not need this time, we used it to great effect much more often. We found this time essential to prepare, share insights and observations, offer mutual support, and think together about students' needs. We also found that the verbal and nonverbal signals we noticed in class faded quickly if we did not explore them soon after each class. This practice helped us attend better to each other and to acknowledge that this material triggers reactions in teachers as well as students.

Providing a student-centered learning environment

Teaching about race and racism is not a singularly intellectual process. In any course, a student-centered approach will address not just cognitive learning but also affective and experiential learning. Our course often elicits emotional and intellectual responses from students and from us. While there is a certain amount of risk inherent in such seminars, they can be personally and intellectually transformative, which is exciting. Therefore, we were committed to pairing the content goals with an equally rigorous approach to the affective and experiential components of learning (in our case, intergroup dialogue process).

Dialogue, group processes, and discussion are key learning activities in our courses. While we have explicit learning outcome goals for each of these activities, there is an art to figuring out together when to introduce a topic, draw out or cut off a perspective, leave a topic or discussion, and linger on it. We have found that it is essential to be flexible—with each other and with our students. We often joke with the song lyrics, "You've got to know when to hold 'em and know when to fold 'em."

Helping students to find the right balance of personal reflection and perspective taking is an art form as well. In our course, we began by asking students to reflect on and share personal experiences. While respecting their personal narratives, we encourage students to understand their individual experiences in the context of aggregate experiences of social groups in society. Our goal is to help students continue to refine their ability to think critically about their values and beliefs while at the same time helping them to understand the perspectives of those who are different from themselves. It is in light of these goals that the case study assignment provided an important opportunity for the exchange of different perspectives, experiences, and applications to emerge (see Appendix B).

Teams

As a team, we share some essential similarities in how we should approach teaching and learning about race and racism. We value equally the process of learning and the content of the course. In addition, it is clear to our students that we both like and learn from each other. To this end, we have agreed on the value of bringing ourselves more fully into the classroom. We describe ourselves more openly and deeply, including our formal preparation, research and community interests, and life experiences (appropriate to our course content, level of students, and learning outcome goals). In doing so, we model the kind of appropriate risks we ask of the class and demonstrate the importance of our personal narratives in understanding the ways we have come to think and act.

Team teaching requires that we collaborate at every step. We had extensive contact before arriving on campus to develop the syllabus, pick readings and videos, and align assignments. Once on campus, we met before every class to confirm plans and respond to current events. Additionally, when possible we met after every session to debrief. If it was not possible to meet in person, we established a regular phone time. We paid particular attention to collaborating on assessment and evaluation responsibilities. Generally, we did most of these tasks together, but some assignments seemed to benefit from independence (for example, responding to student journals).

Recent research has revealed that teams function best when they are balanced, with differences in personal temperament and personality (Ouellett & Fraser, 2005). This research found that interracial teams work best when there is similarity in level of teaching experience and philosophical congruence. Interracial teams need to model equal participation and interaction, and a mentor-mentee teaching team does not provide this equality. This is especially true if the faculty member of color is limited to the role of mentee. Research also finds that four important attributes are essential for effective team teaching: mutual respect, congruence of expectations and flexibility, ability to handle stressors positively, and commitment to dialogue (Ouellett & Fraser, 2005). Therefore, forming compatible, mutually respectful relationships is an essential component of interracial teaching teams.

This leads to our last point, which is that in true team teaching (meaning when both instructors are present and participate equally in every class meeting), there is no room for divas or divos. As we said previously, students have a kind of internal radar that picks up instantly any kind of sustained split between teachers. While this is not necessarily a race- or gender-based conflict, if you add gender and/or race to the mix, it may become even more complicated.

CONCLUSION

Perhaps the most unanticipated outcome of our teaching has been the discovery that, from our students' perspectives, observing our daily interactions and relationship as colleagues was more important to their learning than the formal curriculum. They taught us how important interracial teaching teams can be as models of shared power in the classroom and how they help students to visualize successful, mutually respectful interracial interactions. Moreover, it helps that we like each other and are equally committed to the success of our students and the teaching team.

Finally, we embrace the truth that transformative learning generally takes its own path and time. You may not see progress on the academic calendar timeline; sometimes we only plant the seed. We understand learning about race to be a lifelong process, not a specific destination. Therefore, we focus on building students' sense of efficacy in interracial settings, honing their intergroup dialogue skills, and sharpening their understanding of the value and benefits of a lifelong commitment to social justice in the context of the social work profession.

REFERENCES

Griffin, P. (1997). Facilitating social justice education courses. In M. Adams, L. A. Bell, & P. Griffin (Eds.), *Teaching for diversity and social justice* (pp. 279–298). New York: Routledge.

Marchesani, L. S., & Adams, M. (1992). Dynamics of diversity in the teaching-learning process: A faculty development model for analysis and action. In M. Adams (Ed.), *New directions for teaching and learning, No. 52. Promoting diversity in college classrooms: Innovative responses for the curriculum, faculty, and institutions* (pp. 9–19). San Francisco: Jossey-Bass.

Ouellett, M. L., &. Fraser, E. (2005). Teaching together: Interracial teams. In M. L. Ouellett (Ed.), *Teaching inclusively: Resources for course, department and institutional change in higher education.* Stillwater, OK: New Forums.

Rosenwasser, P. (2000). Tool for transformation: Co-operative inquiry as a process for healing from internalized oppression. In T. Sork, V. L. Chapman, & R. St. Clair (Eds.), *Proceedings of the 41st Annual Adult Education Research Conference* (pp. 392–396). Vancouver, Canada: University of British Columbia, Department of Education Studies, June 2–4.

Appendix A
Racism in the United States:
Implications for Social Work Practice

HBSE 334–3

Smith College School for Social Work Syllabus for HBSE 334–3

Term 1

Instructors: Dr. Edith Fraser & Dr. Mathew Ouellett
Schedule: Mondays and Wednesdays, 8:30 a.m.

Summer 2008

COURSE DESCRIPTION

The nature and impact of racism will be defined and understood from both historical and social structural perspectives. Oppression, prejudice, discrimination, and powerlessness in social and interpersonal contexts will be explored in terms of the social construction of individual and group racial identity and in terms of their impact on individuals, families, groups, and communities. Students will have an opportunity to examine their own experiences of both privilege and oppression. Implications for practice that are strengths-oriented and culturally sensitive will be explored. The unique challenges and particular dilemmas that both students of color and White students encounter in practice will be examined. Students will also learn to critically examine theories, concepts, and models of practice for racial bias. The course will combine lecture, discussion, and experiential learning as students have an opportunity to examine the impact of growing up and living in a racist society and practicing in racist institutions.

The students in this section will have an opportunity to examine their own experiences of both privilege and oppression from the varying perspectives of people of color. The class will explore ways in which internalized oppression in a racist society affects the interaction between individual people of color, the interaction between people of color and White people, as well as the way it affects the interaction among communities of color. Students will draw upon social/historical information and personal experiences of growing up as members of different oppressed populations. They will also examine issues relevant to clinicians of color working with clients from the dominant culture. (Required course second summer, two quarter hours.)

Course Objectives

Upon completion of this course, students should:

1. Develop a beginning knowledge about the historical, social, economic, and global context that has shaped the racial experiences of people of color as well as people from the dominant culture in the U.S.
2. Develop a beginning understanding of concepts and skills that address the impact of individual and institutional racism, prejudice, and discrimination on individuals, families, groups, institutions, and communities from both dominant and targeted groups.
3. Through the process of self-reflection, examine the impact of racism and oppression on their own lives as well as the implications for their careers as clinical social work practitioners.
4. Develop an understanding of the relationship among power, privilege, and oppression and explore the intersection between racism and other forms of systemic oppression.
5. Explore the theories of the social constructions of race, racism, and racial identity development and develop critical thinking skills to evaluate the racial bias embedded in theories and models of practice.
6. Develop a beginning understanding of concepts and skills, social work values and ethics, and strategies for clinical social workers who work collaboratively in their communities to dismantle racism.
7. Develop skills to complete the assessment and implementation of the antiracism project.
8. Develop an understanding of what it means to be clinical social workers of color working within their own communities of color to

develop empowerment skills with clients of color from differing racial and cultural backgrounds.

9. Enhance culturally sensitive clinical skills development of clinicians of color practicing social work with clients from the dominant culture.

Course Format

This course is based on an educational approach that integrates cognitive development with affective aspects of social learning. Our approach encourages students to interact intellectually and emotionally with the information and perspectives presented in class and readings so that new learnings inform the students' professional and social reality more fully. These goals are reflected in how class discussions and written work for the course are designed such as small-group discussions, exercises, presentations, case studies, and videotapes. These will be utilized to examine issues of racism and how they affect one's social work practice.

Course Requirements

In general, you are expected to attend all classes, complete required readings prior to assigned classes, and to actively participate in class discussions and exercises. We require that you keep a weekly journal in which to record reactions, reflections, and analysis related to class discussions, assignments, and readings; a total of four journals are required. You may choose to incorporate personal, professional, and theoretical material into your journal, as well. Please **submit two copies** of your journal each time they are collected for review. Due dates and guidelines for the journal are at the end of the syllabus.

Each student will participate in a small-group project exercise designed as a practice-based case study.

Texts

Required:

Miller, J., & Garran, A. (2007) *Racism in the United States: Implications for the Helping Profession*. Belmont, CA: Thomson/Brooks Coles.

Recommended:

Adams, M., et al. (2000). *Readings for Diversity and Social Justice*. New York: Routledge.

Foster, R., et al. (1996) *Reaching Across Boundaries of Culture and Class.* Lanham, MD: Jason Aronson.

Tatum, B. (1997). *Why Are All of the Black Kids Sitting Together in the Cafeteria.* New York: Basic Books.

Assessment and Evaluation

The criteria for assessment are drawn directly from the previously listed course requirements.

- Attendance
- Participation in discussion, small-group activities, and in-class dialogues
- Evidence of completion of reading assignments in both in-class and out-of-class assignments
- Journal
- Evidence of significant contribution to your small-group case-study assignment
- Listed course requirements

Course plan

Subject to change

1. *Introduction*—Setting the tone for learning and beginning to define the issues
2. *Social Construction of Race and Racism*

Required

Miller, J., & Garran, A. (2007). *Racism in the United States: Implications for the helping profession,* Belmont, CA: Thomson/Brooks Coles, chapters 1, 3, 4.

Race: The Power of an illusion, http://www.pbs.org/race/001_WhatIsRace/001_00home.htm

Journal #1 Due

3. *Racial Identity Development Analysis and Critique*

Readings:

Miller & Garran, chapter 6, pp. 103–131.

Wijeyesinghe, C., & Jackson, B. (2001). *New perspectives on racial identity development.* New York: New York University Press: New York, chapter 7.

4. *Internalized Racism/Intragroup Relations (small group)*

Readings:

Lee, C. A. (2000). An Asian lesbian's struggle. In M. Adams et al. (Eds.), *Readings for diversity and social justice* (pp. 118–120). New York: Routledge.

Padilla, L. (2004). Internalized oppression and Latinos/as. *The Diversity Factor, 12,* 3.

Poupart, L. (2003). The familiar face of genocide: Internalized oppression among American Indians. *Hypatia, 18,* 2.

Rodriguez, R. (2000). *Complexion.* In M. Adams et al. (Eds.), *Readings for diversity and social justice* (pp. 114–118). New York: Routledge.

Recommended:

Anzaldua, G. (1992). En rapport, in opposition: Cobrano cuentas a las nuestras. In A. Rothenberg (Ed.), *Race, class, and gender in the United States.* New York: Worth, p. 408.

Journal #2 Due

5. *Intergroup Relationships* (Come early)

Journal assignment due

Fong, J. (1998). Ethnic conflicts and harmony between African and Asian Americans in the United States. In I. Reed (Ed.), *MultiAmerica: Essays on cultural wars and cultural peace* (pp. 309–318). New York: Penguin.

Payton, B. (1998) *Blacks, browns and yellows at odds.* In I. Reed (Ed.), *MultiAmerica: Essays on cultural wars and cultural peace* (pp. 213–217). New York: Penguin.

Rodriguez, R., & Gonzales, P. (1998). Black/brown relations: An unnecessary conflict. In I. Reed (Ed.), *MultiAmerica: Essays on cultural wars and cultural peace* (pp. 246–257). New York: Penguin.

West, C. (2000). On Black-Jewish relations. In M. Adams et al. (Eds.), *Readings for diversity and social justice* (pp. 177–180). New York: Routledge.

6. *Intergroup Relationships*
7. *Intersections of Oppression*

Readings:

Miller & Garran, chapter 7.
Sacks, K. (1994) How did Jews become white folks? In S. Gregory & R. Sanjek (Eds.), *Race* (pp. 78–102). New Brunswick, NJ: Rutgers University.
Shapiro, J. (2000). A separate and unequal education for minorities with learning disabilities. In M. Adams et al. (Eds.), *Readings for diversity and social justice* (pp. 340–343). New York: Routledge.

Journal #3 Due

Recommended:

Almeida, R., Woods, R., Messino, T., Font, R., & Heer, C. (1994). Violence in the lives of the racially and sexually different: A public and private dilemma. *Journal of Feminist Therapy, 5*(3/4), 99–126.
Greene, B. (1997). Ethnic minority lesbian and gay men: Mental health and treatment issues. In B. Greene (Ed.), *Ethnic and cultural diversity among lesbians and gay men* (pp. 216–240). New York: Sage.
Kaye-Kantrowitz, M. (2000). Jews in the U.S.: The rising cost of whiteness. In M. Adams et al. (Eds.), *Readings for diversity and social justice* (pp. 138–144). New York: Routledge.
Smith, A. (1997) Cultural diversity and the coming-out process. In B. Greene (Ed.), *Ethnic and cultural diversity among lesbians and gay men* (pp. 279–300). New York: Sage.

8. *Implications for Clinical Practice: Case Studies*

Reading:

Miller & Garran, chapter 11, pp. 226–251.

Readings:

Foster, R. (1996). What is a multicultural perspective for psychoanalysis? In R. Foster, M. Moskowitz, & R. Javier (Eds.), *Reaching across boundaries of culture and class* (pp. 3–20). Lanham, MD: Aronson.

Williams, A. (1996). Skin color in psychotherapy. In R. Foster, M. Moskowitz, & R. Javier (Eds.), *Reaching across boundaries of culture and class* (pp. 211–225). Lanham, MD: Aronson.

Recommended Reading:

Comas-Diaz, L. (1994). LatiNegra: Mental health issues of African Latinas. *Journal of Feminist Family Therapy, 5*(3 & 4), 35–74.
Javier, R. (1996). Psychodynamic treatment with the urban poor. In R. Foster, M. Moskowitz, & R. Javier (Eds.), *Reaching across boundaries of culture and class* (pp. 93–114). Lanham, MD: Aronson.

9. Implications for Clinical Practice: Case Studies (cont.)

Readings:

Foster, R. (1996). Assessing the psychodynamic function of language in the bilingual patient. In R. Foster, M. Moskowitz, & R. Javier (Eds.), *Reaching across boundaries of culture and class* (pp. 243–265). Lanham, MD: Aronson.
Gorkin, M. (1996). Countertransference in cross-cultural psychotherapy. In R. Foster, M. Moskowitz, & R. Javier (Eds.), *Reaching across boundaries of culture and class* (pp. 159–178). Lanham, MD: Aronson.
Javier, R. (1996). *In search of repressed memories in bilingual individuals.* In R. Foster, M. Moskowitz, & R. Javier (Eds.), *Reaching across boundaries of culture and class* (pp. 225–243). Lanham, MD: Aronson.

Journal # 4 Due

Recommended:

Pinderhughes, E. (1989). *Assessment and treatment* (chapters 7 and 8). New York: Free Press.

10. Towards an Improved Field of Social Work: Goals and Action Plans

Reading:

Miller & Garran, chapter 13, pp. 275–288.
Collins, P. (2000). Toward a new vision: Race, class, and gender as categories of analysis and connection. In M. Adams et al. (Eds.), *Reading for diversity and social justice* (pp. 457–462). New York: Routledge.

Lourde, A. (1984). Age, race, class and sex: Women redefining difference. In A. Rothenberg (Ed.), *Race, class, and gender in the United States* (pp. 588–595). New York: Worth.

Pharr, S. (2000). Reflections on liberation. In M. Adams et al. (Eds.), *Readings for diversity and social justice* (pp. 450–456). New York: Routledge.

Appendix B
Racism in the United States:
Implications for Social Work Practice

HBSE 334

Dr. Edith Fraser and Dr. Mathew Ouellett

CASE STUDIES AND CLASS PRESENTATIONS

Case studies, descriptions of experiences, and interactions drawn from your own clinical practice will be used in this course to ground our discussions of the historical and theoretical concepts of race and racism to clinical social work. Ideally, each profile will describe an interracial relationship (or interaction) that has left you with unresolved questions about the implications of race and racism in social work practice. Profiles can be drawn from your experiences with peers, supervisors, institutional settings, or clients in your prior clinical placements. By sharing and discussing these profiles, we will provide class participants the opportunity to revisit these experiences and to reframe them in light of the theoretical models introduced in class and the reflections offered by fellow participants.

As a homework assignment, class participants think of an interracial interaction that took place in the context of their social work placement that they would like to discuss.

Step One

Directions:

a. Describe an interaction that took place in the context of your clinical placement where issues of race and/or racism were factors and about which you have unresolved questions. This may be an interaction with a

client, with a colleague (peers or supervisor), or with the institutional setting (policies, procedures, values, expectations) of your placement.
b. Briefly describe your relationships to the individual(s) involved, the nature of the interaction, and your questions.
c. Using chapter 10 (pp. 220, 225), include an assessment of your agency.

Step Two

Directions:

a. Participants self-select into triads.
b. Each participant in the small group briefly presents his or her profile and agency assessment.

Profiles include the following information:

c. Overview of significant factors in the interaction
d. Description of the institutional setting
e. The role of the social worker in this interaction (formal and informal expectations)
f. The questions that remain for the presenter about the interaction.

Note: The role of other participants at this stage of the process is to focus on listening to each report *without* offering feedback, suggestions, or intervention strategies. Questions that clarify the dynamics of the interaction, the relationships involved, or the outcomes described in the profile are helpful and invited.

g. After hearing all three profiles, each small group is next asked to choose one profile from its group to focus upon as a class presentation.

Step Three

Directions:
Each team develops a class presentation of its profile. Presentations include:

a. A brief written description (e.g., one-half to one page typed) of the specific interaction to include, the individuals involved and their roles, the institutional context of the interaction, the key questions about race and / or racism in this interaction, and the role / goals of the social worker.
b. Critical analysis of each profile. Based upon the theoretical models and readings presented in class and the assigned texts, each small group is

asked to decide on three or four questions to be used to focus the large-group discussion on the broader, more universal aspects of their profile. These questions should explore the implications for *antiracist social work practice*, which might be drawn from their profile. For example, "When should a social worker . . .," "How does a social worker . . .," and so on.

c. Open, reflective discussion, lead by the small-group members, is an opportunity to further synthesize concepts, and solicit further insights, suggestions, strategies, and questions for future practice.

Guidelines for Class Presentations

a. Present your case profile as concisely as possible while also providing enough context and background for participants to understand the example.

b. Next, identify the key questions that emerged from it from the perspective of your small group. Especially, questions related to issues of race or racism in this interaction. What were the important questions for your group and why?

c. Describe your group's analysis of the interaction. What values, theories, or models informed your observations and discussions?

d. Explore the implications or new learning that emerged from this discussion and that your group sees as having importance for conducting an antiracist practice as a social worker.

Appendix C
Racism in the United States:
Implications for Social Work Practice

HBSE 334

Dr. Edith Fraser and Dr. Mathew Ouellett

USE OF CAUCUS GROUPS

Caucuses provide students of different racial affinity groups with a forum for interacting and reflecting together to address the group's priority issues. For example, participants in intragroup dialogues might choose to address the effects of internalized oppression or internalized racial superiority. While the general learning outcome goals are the same across groups, the content, questions, and processes in each group may be different.

Within caucus groups, members are often diverse. For example, the person of color group includes students of color from various racial and ethnic groups. They might meet together to understand and confront a range of manifestations of internalized oppression, to develop strategies to become a "rainbow coalition," or to address and dismantle racism on campus and in our agencies. On the other hand, the White caucus group may focus on understanding and confronting issues related to unearned racial privilege, internalized values and assumptions about power, and learning to become White allies.

Caucus groups convene during class several times over the course. On those days, caucuses meet for the first part of the class and then, during the second part, the two groups come together as a team ready to work collaboratively to address racism. The faculty member whose racial identity matches the group's facilitates the caucus but members develop the guidelines and determine the focus of the group.

The caucus group is an integral component and strategy for dismantling racism and becoming an antiracist institution. This is a strategy used by other organizations committed to dismantling racism such as: Cross Roads Ministry; Visions, Inc.; and The People's Institute for Survival and Beyond.

5

Lessons Learned From an Interdisciplinary Course in Undergraduate Science

Ronald J. Duchovic

In the effort to be both an educator and a scholar, the contemporary university faculty member is confronted by a vexing and often perplexing dichotomy. On the one hand, each subdiscipline of human knowledge is a highly integrated body of information with an awesome and sometimes intimidating scope. How is it possible for a traditional college course to delineate a coherent and reasonably complete understanding of any single discipline? On the other hand, faculty members are educators challenged with the responsibility "to lead," but to lead in the sense of "rearing" or "bringing up" or "to raise." This is the root meaning of the term *education*. Every faculty member bears the profound responsibility of guiding fresh, inquisitive minds to become active contributors to and creative originators of their social milieu.

In this context, the education of a human being supersedes the mere transmission of expert knowledge, the simple understanding of specialized technologies, or the initiation of an individual person in arcane mysteries and ceremonies. In particular, the time-honored and well-defined approach of the classroom lecture, literally "reading" to the students, simply fails to encompass adequately the rich and demanding diversity of this dual challenge. Contemporary education must be a process that exemplifies the defining characteristics of humankind and, by this example, empowers students to assume the demanding roles of intellectual and personal leadership.

This empowerment can be achieved through a variety of innovative pathways. One of the great strengths of the current educational milieu has been a willingness to explore alternatives to the traditional college lecture. Here we focus on team teaching, a teaching technique that is both an immersive environment surrounding students and a dynamic learning context actively engaging a community of intellects. The implementation of team teaching in a format that transcends the so-called tag team approach (in which multiple instructors never interact with one another except when parceling out responsibilities for specific parts of a course); explicitly demonstrates the existence of multiple explanatory paradigms; demands the engaged participation of a collection of intellects where both teacher and student become coequal learners; and highlights the interdisciplinary intersection of multiple avenues of human learning.

In what follows, we examine a specific example of team teaching that was developed to present an interdisciplinary view of the physical sciences for students whose major discipline was not a physical science. This specific example is significant for a number of reasons: it involved exploring the nature of physical science; it contributed to the general education mission of the university; it addressed the principle of scientific literacy within a technological society; it demonstrated the limits of various ways of "knowing"; and, finally, it articulated the challenge of educating citizens capable of participation in a broader society. Additionally, our examination of this example highlights practical economic and technological issues associated with a team-teaching approach.

AN INTERDISCIPLINARY SCIENCE COURSE FOR NON-SCIENCE MAJORS

In the early 1990s at Indiana University–Purdue University Fort Wayne (IPFW), we undertook the development of a new course aimed at students whose major was not one of the physical sciences. The course was open to students at all levels, from freshman through those planning to graduate within one academic year. The course required no special preparation or prerequisite background in mathematics or the physical sciences.

The course consisted of four separate modules, each which would be taught by a single faculty member from a specific discipline. Rather than attempting to present a comprehensive overview of a discipline, each module focused on either a single topic or small subset of topics from the discipline. Consequently, the goal of each module was to present a small but characteristic glimpse of four disciplines over the span of two academic semesters. As a result, the course was not content-driven; the goal was not to present an overwhelming mass of integrated information from a single discipline. Rather, the course was process-focused; a much higher priority was placed on the "doing" of science than on the dense content and internal organization and consistency of any single discipline. As a result, the course was structured primarily as a laboratory course.

The year-long course was organized so that two modules were taught each semester. Five distinct modules were developed over a two-year period: Symmetry Module, Chaos Module, Weathering Module, Water Module, and Biology Module (see Appendix A for a sample syllabus for one of these modules). Additionally, each semester began with an introductory module that laid out the tone and broad goals of that particular semester. Each semester closed with a brief capstone segment that reviewed the major issues raised during the semester and reexamined them in light of the entire semester's discussions and activities. The capstone segment was purposefully included to illuminate specific connections among the semester's modules and to highlight not simply the "content" of science but rather the "process" of doing science.

Each module was presented using a mixture of lecture, hands-on activities, and extended in-class discussions. The class met five hours per week, a single one-hour lecture meeting and two two-hour laboratory meetings. While the lecture meeting often focused on specific content, all three presentation formats were used in each class meeting, and central to the discussions was the concurrent presence of all faculty members teaching the modules. Consequently, throughout the two semesters of the course, one faculty member had primary responsibility for each class meeting, but three additional faculty members were present at every class meeting. The simultaneous presence of four faculty members meant that this course was not a tag team effort in which the students saw only one faculty member at a time and in which the simultaneous participation of multiple faculty members occurred during formal planning sessions. The simultaneous presence of four faculty members at each class meeting was a unique identifying characteristic of this course and, as discussed in the following section, stimulated discussions that were unusually animated and wide-ranging.

As noted previously, the class meetings also included a hands-on or interactive component. That is, in addition to a classical lecture component and extended discussions involving both students and multiple faculty members, each class meeting, and especially the laboratory meetings, attempted to engage students in learning activities. Laboratory activities ranged from the simple observation of physical properties, characteristics, or principles to investigating apparently puzzling and anomalous physical behaviors. Students were asked to investigate, analyze, and articulate potential explanations that were consistent with their observations. In effect, the students were invited to engage actively in the process of "doing" science rather than simply being introduced to a long list of well-established physical principles.

Finally, the course incorporated a writing component. The students were required to keep daily journals in which they responded to the class meeting by indicating confusion, amazement, wonder, or any other reaction to the day's presentation. The faculty collected and read the journals and provided the course instructors with a student's view of the course. In effect, the journals encouraged thoughtful reflection by the students, but they also supplied critical feedback to the course instructors concerning the coherence, clarity, and completeness of the course presentation.

This course was offered for two successive academic years from 1992 to 1994. Faculty members from biology, chemistry, geosciences, mathematics, and physics participated as course instructors. Three of six faculty members participated in the course both years (see Duchovic, Maloney, Majumdar, & Manalis, 1998).

SIGNIFICANT CHARACTERISTICS OF THIS TEAM-TEACHING MODEL

It is clear from the brief description given previously that this team-taught course differed significantly in content, presentation, and student participation from a traditional, discipline-specific science course. As a result, the course had a number of unusual characteristics that distinguished it from a traditional science or philosophy of science course.

Nature of Science—Scientific Literacy

First and foremost the course constituted a novel exploration of the nature of science. Yes, the topics visited during the course were all found in other science courses, but the broader picture of science as a "way of knowing or approaching" the universe was the central focus of this course. This broader picture was not simply presented; it was literally demonstrated by the interactions of the scientific panel present for each class presentation. In effect, the students were exposed to, and more critical, participated in discussions whose central focus was the application of scientific principles and scientific reasoning. This exploration of the nature of science in a team-taught environment immediately presented an opportunity to enhance the students' scientific literacy.

Multiple Paradigms

A crucial component of this enhanced scientific literacy was the articulation of multiple scientific paradigms in the course of any single class discussion. Because representatives of several diverse disciplines were all present, each question raised in the class discussion could be examined from the perspective of multiple, discipline-specific paradigms. It was not a question of "the correct" scientific explanation but rather the recognition that there are often multiple, equally valid, and equally cogent explanations for an observed phenomenon. Instructors from different disciplines brought to the class multiple discipline-specific frameworks for addressing the physical universe.

The most critical aspect of the recognition of multiple paradigms lay in the realization that science is not monolithic, presenting only a single explanation, interpretation, or theoretical formulation consistent with the available data. On the one hand, individual disciplines often generate complementary descriptions of a segment of the physical universe. These descriptions mutually support one another without being in any sense identical. On the other hand, individual disciplines can generate descriptions that are both logically consistent and well supported by the available empirical data, but that are distinctly different explanations for a portion of the physical universe. At any given point it may be impossible to choose one explanation over a second or third potential explanation simply because each hypothesis is either equally plausible or equally explanatory.

Again, it is critical to note that the students were not simply "told" about this intersection of the sciences. On the contrary, they participated actively in delineating the multiple paradigms related to their questions and observations. In the class discussions, students became immersed in the multiple, discipline-specific paradigms used in modern science to describe and understand a physical phenomenon. Clearly, the team-teaching component was critical to this immersion.

Scientific Theory

The exposure to multiple scientific paradigms provided a particularly incisive introduction to the nature of scientific theory. The words *theory* and *theoretical* are often understood in common language to mean that an idea is provisional, that it is not well-validated or well-supported. The use of the term *theory* in science stands in strong contradiction to this common use. When a scientific discipline uses the term, it understands a theory to be the explanation most consistent with the entire range of observed phenomena. It is not an idea that can be accepted or rejected with equanimity. While provisional in the sense that a theory can always be falsified, a scientific theory represents the most consistent and comprehensive explanation that is consistent with the available empirical data.

The classroom discussions inevitably led to an examination of multiple, discipline-specific paradigms that provided a variety of theoretical explanations of the same phenomenon. These explanations were rooted in the individual disciplines. The students in the course directly experienced the scientific use of the term *theory* and were often faced with maintaining several simultaneous "theoretical" explanations of the same phenomenon.

Scientific Thinking

Throughout their educational careers, students are introduced to the scientific method. The typical presentation depicts the scientific method as a simple, linear thinking process consisting of a series of well-defined, almost automatic steps. Consequently, the scientific method comes to represent the apex of human thought, a series of invariably correct steps leading to a single, "scientifically" correct conclusion.

This standard introduction has serious flaws. First, the assumption of simple linearity does not reflect the complexity and intricacy of a scientific investigation adequately. Interrogating the universe around us is often a highly nonlinear process. The pursuit of a scientific investigation often necessitates continually revisiting various stages in the investigative process. Second, the assumption that there is a single scientific method, equally applicable under all conditions and to every investigation, simply ignores the amazing diversity of the universe and the rich subtlety of the investigations scientists pursue. For example, scientific investigations are traditionally classified as either theoretical or experimental. In reality, with very few exceptions, no study is purely theoretical or purely experimental. Finally, the advances in computer technology over the last half-century have now made computation and simulation co-equal with theory and experiment as components of scientific investigations.

However, the most glaring limitation of traditional introductions to the scientific method is that students do not participate actively in the method. The method is described, discussed, and dissected in minute detail, but students generally do not actively engage in the "doing" of science. Even the so-called laboratory component of many science courses is simply nothing more than a set of instructions that students follow to demonstrate a particular phenomenon. Laboratory manuals would be more honest in referring to demonstrations rather than experiments.

The team-taught course attempted to remedy this most glaring limitation at two distinct levels. Since each module consisted of lectures, hands-on activities, and discussions, the students experienced and engaged in scientific thinking in two ways. First, the hands-on activities were often open-ended in that specific instructions were not given. The goal was to observe phenomena and draw conclusions, to ask specific questions and attempt to formulate cogent explanations. In effect, the students were invited and encouraged to engage in the process of doing science, not simply discussing the scientific method.

However, what distinguished this course from other hands-on educational environments were the discussions involving both students and the panel of professional scientists that constituted the course instructors. It was here that the team-teaching dimension of the course played a most significant role. In the course of the discussions, students were able to "hear a scientist think." In effect, the faculty panel present at each class meeting actively modeled thinking like a scientist for the students. Similar to the apprenticeships instituted by medieval guilds and continued in a number of professions today, students in this course were the professional scientists' apprentices. They experienced firsthand the crafting of scientific questions and explanations.

But students were not simply observers; they were invited, encouraged, and, in a real sense, required to be participants. They were actively engaged in the discussions, raising questions and proposing explanations. Further, in the journal component of the course, students had an opportunity to reflect on the thinking process in which they had been immersed during the day's class meeting and to think scientifically. In effect, the journal exercise gave the students independent practice in the art of scientific thinking.

General Education

As noted earlier, this interdisciplinary science course encouraged students to expand their scientific literacy. The course very clearly used principles and paradigms from several different disciplines. As a result, students expanded their knowledge base in the sciences by examining and using the principles and theories presented in the course.

However, this course affected another aspect of scientific literacy as well. There has been a renewed emphasis on general education in college and university degree programs. The goal is to provide students with the critical thinking skills that enable educated individuals to solve problems and make informed decisions every day. Further, general education programs also aspire to introduce students to a subset of the panoply of cultures and traditions that differ from their own culture and traditions.

The team-taught interdisciplinary science course contributed strongly to a general education program by challenging students to develop listening, speaking, writing, and quantitative reasoning skills. The discussion component of the classroom presentations demanded that students listen attentively and speak coherently. The journal component required the students to write both effectively and reflectively about the discussion topics. Finally, in the course of class discussions, two distinct dimensions of quantitative reasoning emerged. First, students were immersed in the thinking of active physical scientists. A hallmark of modern science since the 17th century has been the use of increasingly quantitative models to describe the universe. The students directly experienced scientists' use of these models in the course of the class discussions. Second, the students not only were exposed to the reasoning processes of active scientists, but they also were engaged in the active use of that reasoning as they participated in the discussion. Since the discussions occurred with the participation of professional scientists, the students received immediate feedback on the quality of their reasoning. This again demonstrates the apprenticeship character of this team-taught course and its impact on the development of the students' quantitative reasoning capability.

Scientific Intimidation

The very nature of the scientific enterprise often generates a sense of overwhelming intimidation in the novice practitioner or nonspecialist. The various physical science disciplines are dominated by two conspicuous characteristics. First, they are data dense—that is, over the four centuries since the advent of modern science, an impressive (some might say *oppressive*) compendium of observations of the physical universe has been accumulated and codified. For the neophyte, this mass of information presents a daunting web of interconnected complexity. At first glance, rather than bringing a sense of order and connectedness to the physical universe, the collected information seems unnecessarily convoluted. The level of detail and the multiple interconnections present an apparently unmanageably complex amount of information that may seem impossible to master.

Second, over the past 400 years, the physical sciences have become increasingly mathematical. Beginning with Newtonian physics and continuing through chemistry and, today, the modern life sciences, mathematics and the powerful reasoning associated with abstract mathematics have become the hallmarks of modern science. This strongly mathematical flavor of the sciences is another intimidating characteristic that often dampens the spirit of the novice approaching science or a particular scientific discipline for the first time. This stumbling block is complicated further because mathematics is a large and complex field in its own right, requiring considerable time and effort to achieve simple competence in, let alone mastery of, even one small part of a vast subject. Yet, competence in (and often mastery of) mathematics is a prerequisite for the initial approach to a scientific discipline.

In the case of this course, the level of intimidation was exacerbated by the mere presence of a group of scientific experts in the classroom. Each faculty member who was part of the teaching team represented often decades of accumulated scientific expertise. This fact was not lost on the students. At the beginning, they were hesitant to raise questions or volunteer tentative explanations out of fear of being wrong or looking silly. Consequently, careful consideration was given to breaking the ice and inviting the students to participate as early as possible in the interactive character of the course.

Although somewhat of a paradox, it was possible to turn the high level of expertise the faculty panel represented into a vehicle that reduced the students' level of intimidation. While each faculty member represented a high level of expertise in his or her own particular discipline, the very structure of modern science with its attention to detail and its emphasis on narrow specialization meant that the experts were generally ignorant of other disciplines. The team teaching reduced the students' apprehensions by pointing out that a chemist was not necessarily an expert in biology, or that a physicist was not necessarily an expert in geosciences.

This desired result did not occur automatically. Faculty participating in the course made a conscious decision to minimize the tendency to be self-assured, some might say arrogant, when presenting a particular point of view during a discussion. While faculty members made their perspective known in a concise and carefully reasoned manner, they made no attempt to trivialize the points being made. Disagreements did occur, and distinct, discipline-specific interpretations emerged. However, the discussions were invariably civil and nonjudgmental, allowing students the opportunity to participate. In this way, the team-teaching format encouraged students to develop their thinking and to propose interpretations and explanations. In effect, the students experienced the freedom to participate in the scientific process and seemed to overcome their initial apprehension of not knowing enough to be part of the discussion.

It is clear, however, that team teaching is not a panacea for the other dimensions that make the physical sciences so intimidating. We ameliorated the issue of data density somewhat by focusing on only a small subset of topics rather than attempting a comprehensive discussion of dozens of individual topics. This was somewhat successful, but it did not eliminate the fact that each faculty member had succeeded in mastering a staggering amount of the "stuff" of science.

Several of the modules were also overtly mathematical. Consequently, there was no attempt to remove mathematics from the presentations; however, the mathematics did not become the central focus of either presentations or discussions. Every effort was made to use the mathematics to enlighten and to expand the presentations or analyses. In this way, students saw mathematics as a useful tool rather than a barrier to understanding the process of science.

Complete Descriptions of Reality

The contemporary media often present "scientific" data and accompanying theories as the most trustworthy forms of human knowledge. In the popular view, after a proposition has been "scientifically demonstrated" it is not open to further examination. Associated with this sense of finality is the further assumption that there are no disagreements among scientists, no contradictory interpretations of the same data set. This view arises partly from the nature of science itself. One of the defining characteristics of science is its unwavering drive to eliminate logical contradictions and interpretational disagreements about the universe around us (see Quinn, 2009). In fact, when viewing the history of western science, one sees that the many significant paradigm shifts occurred at those junctures when inconsistencies were finally resolved. However, as we note shortly, this is not the complete story.

Galileo's observation of the moons of Jupiter and the phases of Venus provided observational data that were inconsistent with the Ptolemaic universe and a stationary earth located at its center. Over a span of slightly more than a hundred years (aided by the further work of Kepler and Newton), the sun-centered model of the universe governed by Newtonian gravitation became the dominant astronomical paradigm, resolving the inconsistency. An understanding of the origin of disease required a very long period of investigation during which various potential explanations were discarded in the face of contradictory evidence. While a germ theory explaining the origin of disease had been advanced by the first third of the 19th century, it was only after the work of Pasteur and Robert Koch that the germ theory was adopted as the modern paradigm explaining disease processes.

These two examples demonstrate the most common resolution of inconsistencies: careful observations were collected over time, and one of a number of competing paradigms emerged as the most successful explanation of the studied phenomena. However, this sequence of events is, in a very real sense, an example of the least interesting paradigm shift that has occurred in the sciences. A much more fascinating "revolution" occurs when entirely new points of view emerge in the resolution of an extant inconsistency. These new points of view enforce an alternative understanding of the basic structure and properties of the physical universe.

In one of his stunning 1905 papers, Albert Einstein confronted what had become known as the "moving magnet and conductor problem." The crucial point of Einstein's analysis was that the same experimental observable, an electric current in a conductor, arises from two entirely different descriptions—in one case a magnetic field, in the other case an electric field. This asymmetrical description led Einstein to formulate an entirely new conception of our reality. To remove the apparent inconsistency, Einstein proposed two basic postulates: The Principle of Relativity and The Principle of a Constant Speed of Light.

Einstein's ideas revolutionized the fundamental and long accepted concepts of space, time, and simultaneity. Time and space are not independent and absolute; simultaneity depends on the relative uniform motion of the observer. A completely different order of paradigm shift occurred as a result of Einstein's work. It was a shift in the underlying basic assumptions made in multiple areas of human thought, changing forever the critical starting points humankind had used to understand the universe.

The development of quantum theory is another paradigm shift of monumental proportions. It established a new model for the microscopic structure of the universe, resolving glaring inconsistencies between existing theoretical models and a large body of observational data and providing a new mathematical framework with which to view the microscopic universe. Just as the special theory of relativity introduced novel views of space, time, and simultaneity, quantum theory makes discreteness, probability, indeterminacy, and nonlocality the new categories of thought for the contemporary world.

The first two paradigm shifts summarized previously seem to reinforce the popular understanding of science. Once the definitive experiment is complete, there is no need to reexamine or question the conclusions. An old paradigm is replaced by a new paradigm. However, this simplistic view of the scientific process changed dramatically with the dawn of the 20th century. The special theory of relativity and quantum theory were watersheds in which the paradigm shifts affected multiple areas of human thought. The most basic assumptions about the structure of the universe simply changed. The paradigm shift introduced by quantum theory is even more problematic.

Over the quarter-century it took to develop quantum theory, there was no single, definitive experiment that highlighted an inconsistency resolved by the adoption of the theory. Rather, quantum theory evolved through a series of steps that successfully explained or interpreted multiple experimental data sets. Consequently, the quantum theory paradigm shift introduced a new dimension that stands in further contradiction to the popular notion of the finality of a so-called scientific explanation. Even after a century, there is no unanimous agreement about humankind's interpretation of the meaning of the quantum theory. In fact, there are multiple competing interpretations of the theory, and discussion of it continues among contemporary physicists.

This brief summary of paradigm shifts in science demonstrates that modern science is far from the monolithic leviathan often presented in popular discussions. The "simple" process of resolving inconsistencies and proceeding from one paradigm to a revised paradigm in a straightforward, linear progression is an idealization not supported by the history of modern science. It is a myth that there is only a single explanation at any given time in a particular scientific discipline; it is more frequently the case that there are disagreements and vigorous arguments about a particular paradigm.

One of the powerful strengths of this team-taught course was the active demonstration to the students that disagreements do exist, that different disciplines may not share the same paradigm explaining observed phenomena, and that science is not simply a massive body of indisputable "facts" but rather is a "process of discovery." Not only do individual disciplines offer distinct and often differing interpretations of experimental data, but there also can be vigorous disagreement about an explanation or interpretation of the data. As a result of the discussions among the faculty members participating in the course, students were able to observe the "process" of science. They witnessed firsthand the development of explanations. They heard the disagreements that arose from discipline-specific interpretations of a data set. Finally, they actively participated in this "process" of science by engaging in the discussions themselves rather than being told about or simply hearing disagreements.

EDUCATING CITIZENS

A tension exists in our universities and colleges between the creation of new knowledge (the research dimension) and the critical role of the university as the transmitter and disseminator of both novel and well-established knowledge (the teaching dimension). While American research universities have an enviable and well-deserved identity as engines of remarkable intellectual development, pushing the boundaries of human knowledge in the arts and sciences, the vast majority of their graduates will be primarily citizens living in a clearly demarcated cultural setting. As such, the teaching dimension of higher education, the process of preparing citizens to live productively and ethically within a society, cannot be merely a tangential thread in the tapestry of higher education. To do so is to put the integrity of our society at risk; by ignoring the importance of excellent teaching, we imperil our future (Colby, Ehrlich, Beaumont, & Stephens, 2003).

The challenge, then, is to create a rich amalgam in which both educators and students participate in a community that is characterized by the very best qualities of human scholarship. This community, however, cannot be merely an assembly of outstanding technicians who are skilled in the specialized intricacies of the various technologies that abound in our society. On the contrary, the members of this community of scholars must be thoughtful individuals, capable of comprehensive, integrative, and critical thinking. They must have come to love knowledge and are capable of learning for a lifetime.

In the early 1990s, these considerations were not consciously part of the planning for a team-taught course. However, the characteristics of the course discussed here are precisely the characteristics educated citizens require. The ability to think comprehensively, integratively, and critically rests on recognizing that any single scientific discipline, and more generally science itself as a way of knowing, is fundamentally a process rather than a simple compendium of data. The crucial element that a team-teaching environment (in the form described previously) possesses is the characteristic of "process." The course did not focus on a single discipline but rather, through a series of individual modules, introduced students to the "doing" of science. This was reinforced by both the reflective writing and the discussion components of the course. Again, it cannot be overstated that the presence of a panel of faculty members who participated with students in the discussions made the "doing" of science the central characteristic of this course.

As a result of the modular structure centered on the discussions, students were challenged to think comprehensively. That is, thinking was never left at the discipline-specific level because every discussion engaged multiple disciplines. Each topic and hands-on investigation was pursued integratively because experts from multiple disciplines simultaneously engaged in the discussions among themselves and with the students. Finally, critical thinking was an absolute requirement for effective and substantial participation in the discussions; it was central to effective reflective writing.

Finally, the team-teaching environment engendered a love of knowledge simply through the spirited and spontaneous nature of the discussion. The discussions were not formulaic, following a well-scripted outline. Quite to the contrary, the discussions were not planned in advance, and they were not scripted to reach a predetermined goal or terminus. They were open-ended and wide-ranging, characterized by spontaneity tempered with mutual respect. In retrospect, the discussions were lively, boiling cauldrons out of which emerged understanding and insight. There is no better environment for instilling a love of knowledge and the desire to remain a lifelong learner.

The role of educating citizens to participate actively and creatively in their society is not one of secondary importance. It is, in fact, a role of central importance to that society. The team-teaching environment discussed here is a highly effective tool for educating citizens. No society can endure if its citizens do not assume both moral and civic responsibility for their actions.

LESSONS LEARNED

As noted previously, the team-taught course was offered for two years. Given the scope and range of its potential impact, one must ask: "Why only two years?" The simplest answer is: practicality. It was not an effective use of faculty to engage five of them over two semesters for approximately 20 students. The course was simply not cost-effective. While it admirably achieved many of its goals, the course was not sustainable in face of the costs in time and money.

In the almost two decades that have passed since the course was first offered, a number of technological innovations have occurred that conceivably would affect its structure. The journaling exercise could now be done electronically, making them available to both the faculty and the whole class, so class members could review and respond reflectively outside of class meetings to the observations their fellow students made and the questions they posed. This would introduce a new dimension to the course's reflective thinking component.

Complementing the individual student journals, modern technology would allow for peer-reviewed essays in the course. The use of electronic preparation, submission, and review of student essays would enable students to participate in reviewing essays. Each student could be challenged to write, in a more formal setting than a journal, on a scientific topic and then to evaluate critically the writing of fellow students. Such an exercise would focus attention on the dual skills of communicating clearly in the written word and evaluating critically the writing of another. The evaluation process could be extended very easily to include comments from the faculty panel.

In addition to electronic journals and peer-reviewed essays, modern computer technology would make chat rooms available to class members. In effect, discussions would not necessarily be limited to specific class meeting times; they would now be extended in both time and space. The greater scheduling flexibility introduced by the use of a chat room would address the earlier practical limitations in offering a team-taught course. A chat room session could be initiated anytime during a 24-hour period, which would minimize the difficulties associated with scheduling faculty attendance at discussions. Additionally, the use of a chat room system would introduce the flexibility of scheduling a combination of both in-class and chat room discussions.

A broad range of videoconferencing tools are also available that go beyond the limitations of a chat room environment. While a chat room is usually limited to textual communication, a videoconference would allow everyone to hear the tone and inflections of a respondent's comments, and it would display facial responses and accompanying body language, all of which are important aspects of human communication. Again, videoconferencing would introduce flexibility and improve the practicality of offering a team-taught course.

A videoconferencing environment also means that the teaching team would not be limited to faculty members from a single campus. It would also be possible to include students from multiple campuses or multiple institutions in the course. In fact, the course could take on both an international and cross-cultural dimension that was not even remotely considered some two decades ago. Such a perspective would allow inclusion of a panel of international experts on the teaching team. A multiple campus or multiple institution approach has an added practical benefit; it would address the question of cost effectiveness raised earlier, because no single institution would be responsible for the entire cost of this course. The cost, defined in terms of faculty members committed to the course, would be shared by multiple campuses or institutions.

CONCLUDING REMARKS

There is, in our society, a certain fascination with "novelty" or "newness," a fascination that often assumes an existence that is independent of need or impact. As a result, a novel approach or an innovative technique often is initiated simply because it is new and different. Just because team-taught courses are not the norm is not a compelling reason to create one. However, as has been argued, there are strong and well-founded reasons to adopt a team approach to teaching a course. Further, the team approach articulated and advocated here is not a tag team format, but rather a highly interactive and integrative collaboration of a number of experts.

Faced with the dual responsibility of presenting a coherent description of an integrated body of human knowledge and encouraging creative contributions to a social milieu, the contemporary educator confronts a truly monumental challenge. It is a challenge that can be perceived simultaneously as both discouraging and exhilarating. The additional dimension of educating citizens who readily shoulder moral and civic responsibility imposes an imperative that college and university faculty members often ignore. To do so is to imperil the integrity and viability of human society.

Given this understanding of the multiple dimensions of a modern university education, the team-taught course offers a powerful and highly effective technique to achieve these multiple goals. The ability of this team-taught course to examine the fundamental nature of physical science, to contribute to the general education mission of the university, to address the principle of scientific literacy within a technological society, and to demonstrate the limits of various ways of "knowing" clearly demonstrates that team teaching is a multifaceted and highly effective approach to the challenge of informing citizens about their moral and civic responsibility within the broader society. The variety and richness of the components possible within the framework of a team-taught course strongly recommend it as a premier example of education in its most fundamental sense of "raising up" the future generations who will be our successors.

REFERENCES

Colby, A., Ehrlich, T., Beaumont, E., Stephens, J., & Shulman, L. S. (2003). *Educating citizens: Preparing America's undergraduates for lives of moral and civic responsibility*. San Francisco: Jossey-Bass.

Duchovic, R. J., Maloney, D. P., Majumdar, A., & Manalis, R. S. (1998). Teaching science to the non-science major: An interdisciplinary approach. *Journal of College Science Teaching, 27*, 258–262.

Quinn, H. (2009, July). What is science? *Physics Today, 60*, 8–9.

Appendix A
FWAS 111: Interdisciplinary Natural Science
Symmetry in Science and the Arts

FALL SEMESTER, 1993 IPFW
Dr. Ronald J. Duchovic

I.   Symmetry: A Case of Complements and Contrasts
  a. The Pythagoreans: Music
    i. Simple patterns
       1. The octave
       2. Scales
       3. Physical properties of wind and string instruments
    ii. Classical Music: The Fugue
  b. The Pythagoreans: Architecture
    i. Classical Greek architecture
       1. Golden Mean
    ii. Egyptian architecture and mensuration
       1. Pyramids
       2. Pythagorean theorem
  c. Activities
    i. Fort Wayne Philharmonic
    ii. Video: *Donald Duck in Mathemagic Land*
    iii. Construction of stringed instruments
    iv. Listening
    v. Indiana University—Purdue University Fort Wayne campus architecture

II. Symmetry: Beauty in Intent and Design
  a. Art
    i. Classical painting

   ii. Renaissance art

   iii. Themes in modern art

   iv. Activities

     1. Fort Wayne Art Institute

  b. Literature

   i. Poetry

     1. Meters

     2. Sonnets

     3. Haiku

   ii. Plays and playwrights

     1. Mystery and Morality Plays

     2. Tragedy

     3. Comedy

   iii. Parallelism in literature

     1. Biblical passages

     2. Abraham Lincoln

   iv. Modern novel

   v. Activities

     1. Examples of various poetic meters

     2. Examples from literature

III. Symmetry: Creating the Abstract

  a. Mathematics

   i. Function theory

     1. Even/odd functions

     2. Graphs and special functions

     3. Trigonometric

     4. Parabolic

     5. Hypberbolic

     6. Exponential

     7. Spiral

     8. Helix

   ii. Simple Geometry

     1. Axis of symmetry

     2. Plane of symmetry

     3. Center of symmetry

     4. Axis of improper rotation

     5. Platonic solids

   iii. Abstract algebra

     1. Group theory—geometry revisited

          2. Symmetry operations

          3. Identity

          4. N-fold rotation

          5. Reflection

          6. Inversion

          7. Improper rotation

       iv. Activities

          1. Computer graphics: Platonic or regular polyhedra

          2. Computer generated fractals

          3. Molecular models

          4. 1,3,4,7-tetramethycyclooctoatetraene (S_4)

  b. Natural Sciences

       i. Mathematization of the natural sciences

          1. Astronomy

          2. Physics

          3. Chemistry

          4. Biology

          5. Geosciences

      ii. Interaction of theory and experiment

     iii. Conservation laws

          1. Mass/energy

          2. Momentum (Linear and Angular)

          3. Charge

          4. Parity

      iv. Activities

          1. Steno's Law: Macroscopic crystals

          2. Helium spectrum

          3. Demonstration of angular momentum

IV.   Symmetry in Modern Science

  a. Three Models—Concept of ACTION

       i. Newtonian (Newton)

      ii. Local field (Faraday, Maxwell)

     iii. Minimum Principle (Fermat, Lagrange, Hamilton)

  b. Noether's theorem

       i. Symmetry with respect to action

      ii. Relationship to conservation laws

  c. Activities

       i. Handout: Biochemistry and chirality, from *Science*

      ii. Handout: Search for the Top Quark, from *American Scientist*

V.   Physics
   a. Cosmological Perspective: Special and General Relativity
      i.   Space and time
         1. Newton
         2. Einstein
      ii. Matter and energy
         1. Classical view
         2. Relativity
         3. Combined conservation law
      iii. Gravity and acceleration
         1. Equivalence principle
         2. Gravity as geometry
      iv. Activities
         1. Examine the experimental evidence: Solar eclipse
   b. Atomic Perspective: Quantum Theory
      i.   Particles and waves
         1. Classical view
         2. Quantum electrodynamics
         3. Classical and quantal action
      ii. Reality and locality

VI. Chemistry
   a. Group Theory and Spectroscopy
      i.   Symmetry and observation
      ii. Character tables
   b. Activities
      i.   Laser, infrared, NMR spectroscopy
      ii. Polarimetry
      iii. Smelling chiral compounds

VII. Additional Topics
   a. Subatomic Perspective: Particle Physics
      i.   Symmetry and conservation laws
         1. Application of Noether's theorem
      ii. Particles and Forces
         1. Quark model—quantum chromodynamics
      iii. Activities
         1. Examine the experimental evidence: Top quark?
         2. Paramagnetic phenomena: electron spin

    b. Crystallography
       i. Macroscopic crystal patterns
         1. Point groups
         2. Space groups
       ii. Quasicrystals
         1. A new interpretation
       iii. Fractals
    c. Biochemistry
       i. Enzymes and substrates
         1. Symmetry and function
       ii. Protein geometry and immunology

Suggested Reading:

Altman, S. L. (1992). *Icons and symmetrics*. Oxford, UK: Oxford University Press.

Feynman, R. (1967). *The character of physical law: The 1964 messenger lectures*. Cambridge, MA: MIT Press.

Gregory, B. (1988). *Inventing reality: Physics as language*. New York: Wiley.

Kuhn, T. S. (1990). *The structure of scientific revolutions* (2nd ed.). Chicago: University of Chicago Press.

Wilczek, F., & Devine, B. (1989). *Longing for the harmonics: Themes and variations from modern physics*. New York: W. W. Norton.

Zee, A. (1986). *Fearful symmetry: The search for beauty in modern physics*. New York: Macmillan.

Papers:

Requirements:

Papers must be typewritten
Length: 2–5 pages (500–1,300 words)
Papers must correctly utilize standard English grammar and standard spelling.
Late papers will not be accepted.

Topic for Paper I:

Suppose symmetry did *not* exist in our world. How would the world be different? How would life in an unsymmetrical world be different from your present life?

Topic for Paper II:

Choose *one* symmetry property from art, music, architecture, or literature and discuss its relationship to a modern theory or theories in physics and chemistry. You may use lecture notes and the suggested readings as the basis of your discussion.

VIII. Activities
   a. Attend one concert of the Fort Wayne Philharmonic or listen to three classical recordings (one concerto, one symphony, one composition of your choice)
   b. Video of *Donald Duck in Mathmagic Land*
   c. Construction of stringed instruments
   d. Visit the Fort Wayne Art Institute
   e. Observe campus architecture
   f. Examples from literature—poetic meters
   g. Computer graphics—platonic or regular polyhedra
   h. Computer generated fractals
   i. Molecular models
   j. 1,3,5,7-tetramethylcyclooctatetraene (S_4)
   k. Steno's Law: Macroscopic crystals
   l. Crookes tube; helium/hydrogen spectra
   m. Demonstration of Angular Momentum
   n. Handout: Biochemistry and Chirality, from *Science*
   o. Handout: Search for the Top Quark, from *American Scientist*
   p. Experimental observations from physics
      1. Solar eclipse
      2. Electron spin—paramagnetism
   q. Laser, infrared, NMR spectroscopy
      1. Polarimetry
      2. Smelling chiral molecules

Contributors

Ronald J. Duchovic, associate professor of chemistry at Indiana University–Purdue University Fort Wayne, is a theoretical physical chemist who uses mathematical models on supercomputers to study molecular reaction dynamics and chemical kinetics. He combines these interests with scholarly teaching, allowing him the opportunity both to explore the universe we share and to nurture in others a genuine curiosity about that universe.

Edith Fraser, chair and professor of the Social Work Department at Alabama A & M University, has been in social work education for more than 25 years, and has taught at Alabama A & M, Oakwood University, and Smith School for Social Work. She has served in various academic roles: teacher, director of field practicum, chair of the Social Work Department, and director of faculty development and research.

Amy Jessen-Marshall, associate professor of biology and dean of University Programs at Otterbein University, has been a member of the Otterbein faculty for 10 years. Dr. Jessen-Marshall finds the most interesting "places" to teach are at the intersections of disciplines. Beyond the multiple team-taught courses on Origins: Evolution and Astrobiology, she has taught courses ranging from Cell Biology and Microbiology for Majors to Feminist Evolutionary Theory and Gender and Biology for Women's Studies, in addition to courses for Integrative Studies on Plagues and Pandemics.

Halard L. Lescinsky is professor and chair of the Department of Biology and Earth Science at Otterbein University in Westerville, Ohio. Dr. Lescinsky is a paleontologist and coral reef geologist who is interested in the evolution of marine communities through geologic time. He has chaired the Environmental Studies Program and leads a coral reef ecology course to Belize and a field geology course to Nevada and California. He is currently adapting the "Origins" discussed in chapter 1 into a freshman year seminar.

Min-Ken Liao, professor in the Biology Department at Furman University, teaches biology and specializes in bacteriology and genetics. In addition to laboratory research, Dr. Liao is interested in undergraduate education in microbiology and the scholarship of teaching and learning.

Mathew L. Ouellett is associate director, Center for Teaching and Faculty Development, at the University of Massachusetts Amherst. Dr. Ouellett has taught alone and as part of interracial teaching teams in the School of Education at the university and in the Smith College School for Social Work for more than 20 years. Most recently, he edited *An Intersectional Analysis Approach to Diversity in the College Classroom* for the Jossey-Bass series, New Directions for Teaching and Learning.

Kathryn M. Plank is associate director of the University Center for the Advancement of Teaching and adjunct assistant professor of Educational Policy & Leadership at The Ohio State University. She received her PhD in English from The Pennsylvania State University and currently teaches a graduate course on college teaching. Her research interests include program assessment, teaching consultation, diversity, critical thinking, educational technology, and team teaching.

Robert A. Richter is director of arts programming at Connecticut College, where he directs the onStage at Connecticut College performing arts series and artist residency programs. He is also a Eugene O'Neill scholar and has taught courses on O'Neill, along with Performing Arts in Cultural Context and Arts and Community.

Margaret E. Thomas is an associate professor at Connecticut College, where she also chairs the Music Department. In addition to teaching courses in music theory, she coordinates the Music Student Community Service program and is active on campus-wide committees.

Sarah Worth is an associate professor of philosophy at Furman University. Dr. Worth teaches philosophy and specializes in aesthetics and ancient philosophy. Recently she has been involved in the Biology Department, team teaching three different courses with biologists in neuroscience, disease, and sustainability.

Index

grading issues
  Arts and Community course, 60,
    66–67
  FYS course, 48, 51–52
  and student assessment, 25–26
  and team teaching, 8–9
  and writing assignments, 46
grant funds
  for Arts and Community course, 55
  for FYS course, 38–39
  objectives of, 17–18
  for Origins course, 14, 23
  for social work course, 74
Griffin, P., 75

hands-on activities
  for FYS course, 39, 45
  open-ended, 103
  for Origins course, 15, 16, 28
  for science course, 99
Haynes, C., 15
HIV and AIDS, 45
hominids, 21
human intelligence, evolution of, 21

Indiana University-Purdue University
    Fort Wayne (IPFW), 98
Innovations in Interdisciplinary Teaching,
    15
Integrative Studies program
  and curriculum issues, 14, 16, 17, 18
  goals for, 16
  Origins course as part of, 14
interdisciplinary course(s)
  at Furman University, 38–48
  at Otterbein, 13–28
  and team teaching, 3, 9
  way to teach, 38–39
interdisciplinary science course. *see also*
    science course(s)
  and educated citizens, 108–110
  features of, 100–108
  lectures, 97, 99, 103
  lessons learned from, 110–111
  modules of, 98

for non-science majors, 98–100
  sample syllabus, 113–118
  writing assignments for, 100
intergroup dialogues
  addressing conflicts with, 77
  and caucus groups, 78
  and social work course, 74, 82
intergroup relationships, 87–88
internalized oppression, 75, 87, 94
interracial team teaching. *see* team
    teaching
intragroup relations, 87

Jessen-Marshall, Amy, 16
jigsaw exercises, 24, 25
Johnson, Steven, 43
journal entries, 65, 103, 110

Koch, Robert, 106
Krathwohl, D. R., 3

lab exercises
  FYS course, 39, 47
  Origins course, 21–24
  questionnaire for, 50
  science course, 99, 102
learning environment, 50, 76, 80
lectures
  Arts and Community course, 57
  FYS course, 39–42
  Origins course, 14, 19–21
  related to writing, 46
  science course, 97, 99, 103
Lescinsky, Hal, 16
Liao, Min-Ken, 38
Lyman Allyn Museum, 69

Majumdar, A., 100
malaria, 45
Maloney, D. P., 100
Manalis, R. S., 100
Manoff Center for Teaching and
    Learning, 71
Marchesani, L. S., 75
Marton, F., 3

Cooperative Learning in Higher Education
Across the Disciplines, Across the Academy
Edited by Barbara J. Millis

Research has identified cooperative learning as one of the ten High Impact Practices that improve student learning.

If you've been interested in cooperative learning, but wondered how it would work in your discipline, this book provides the necessary theory, and a wide range of concrete examples.

Experienced users of cooperative learning demonstrate how they use it in settings as varied as a developmental mathematics course at a community college, and graduate courses in history and the sciences, and how it works in small and large classes, as well as in hybrid and online environments. The authors describe the application of cooperative learning in biology, economics, educational psychology, financial accounting, general chemistry, and literature at remedial, introductory, and graduate levels.

The chapters showcase cooperative learning in action, at the same time introducing the reader to major principles such as individual accountability, positive interdependence, heterogeneous teams, group processing, and social or leadership skills.

Also available:

Lesson Study
Using Classroom Inquiry to Improve Teaching and Learning in Higher Education
Bill Cerbin
Foreword by Pat Hutchings

"This volume offers guiding principles, theoretical underpinnings, fresh thinking, detailed examples, and, importantly, a window into the larger community that is now assembling itself around this important work. This is not only a book about lesson study but about teaching and learning more broadly. A deceptively simple process, lesson study opens a wide door to a generous set of understandings and experiences."—*Pat Hutchings*

This is the first book about lesson study for higher education. Based on the idea that the best setting in which to examine teaching is where it takes place on a daily basis—the lecture hall, seminar room, studio, lab, and the online classroom management system—lesson study involves several instructors jointly designing, teaching, studying, and refining an individual class lesson in order to explore student learning problems, observe how students learn, and analyze how their instruction affects student learning and thinking. The primary purpose is to help teachers better understand how to support student learning and thinking. By observing how students learn through lesson study teachers can improve their own teaching and build knowledge that can be used by other teachers to improve their practice.

Focusing on a single lesson enables participants to examine in detail every step of the teaching process, from vision and goals, to instructional design, to implementation, to observation and analysis of student performance, and then evidence-based improvement. It enables faculty to explore learning problems that matter most to them, learn alternative ways to teach from one another, and co-design new course materials.

22883 Quicksilver Drive
Sterling, VA 20166-2102

Subscribe to our e-mail alerts: www.Styluspub.com

Also in the New Pedagogies and Practices for Teaching in Higher Education series:

Series Editor: James Rhem, editor of the premier higher education newsletter, *The National Teaching and Learning Forum*

Each volume of the series presents a specific pedagogy. The editors and contributors introduce the reader to the underlying theory and methodology, provide specific guidance in applying the pedagogy, and offer case studies of practice across a several disciplines, usually across the domains of the sciences, humanities, and social studies, and, if appropriate, professional studies.

Blended Learning
Across the Disciplines, Across the Academy
Edited by Francine Glazer
Foreword by James Rhem

The book constitutes a practical introduction to blended learning—typically involving activities half of which take place face-to-face in a classroom, and half online—illustrated by implementations across a broad spectrum of disciplines. It enables faculty unfamiliar with this mode to address the core challenge of blended learning—which is to link the activities in each medium so that they reinforce each other to create a single, unified, course—and offers models they can adapt.

This book takes two findings as its point of departure. First, that online learning, and blended learning in particular—when they incorporate active-learning strategies, including opportunities for reflection and interaction with peers—can result in significantly better student learning than can be achieved in the conventional classroom. Second, that because they can provide repeated opportunities for students to devote more time on review of information and practice of skills, courses with both synchronous and asynchronous components—for example, blended courses—report more positive outcomes than do courses that are entirely synchronous or entirely asynchronous.

Francine Glazer and the contributors to this book describe how they integrate a wide range of pedagogical approaches in their blended courses; and how they use groups to build learning communities and make the online environment attractive to students. They illustrate under what circumstances particular tasks and activities work best online or face-to-face, and when to incorporate synchronous and asynchronous interactions. They introduce the concept of "layering" the content of courses to ensure that students see both the online and the face-to-face components as equal in value, and devote equal effort to both modalities; and to appropriately sequence material for beginning and experienced learners. The underlying theme of the book is to encourage students to develop the skills to continue learning throughout their lives.

Team Teaching
Across the Disciplines, Across the Academy
Edited by Kathryn M. Plank

For those considering adopting team teaching, or interested in reviewing their own practice, this book offers an overview of this pedagogy, its challenges and rewards, and a rich range of examples in which teachers present and reflect upon their approaches.

Each of the five examples in this book shares the story of a course at a different institution, and each is designed to reflect a number of different variables in team-taught courses. They represent courses in a variety of different disciplines, including the sciences, social sciences, humanities, and the arts; and at a range of levels, from first-year seminars to graduate courses. They also illustrate a number of different models for instructional teams, such as faculty from the same disciplines, from related disciplines, from two very different disciplines, from different institutions, and one pairing of a faculty member and a staff member.

This book provides insight into the impact of team teaching on student learning and on faculty development. It also addresses the challenges, both pedagogical and administrative, that need to be addressed for team teaching to be effective.

Just-in-Time Teaching
Across the Disciplines, and Across the Academy
Edited by Scott Simkins and Mark Maier

Just-in-Time Teaching (JiTT) is a pedagogical approach that requires students to answer questions related to an upcoming class a few hours beforehand, using an online course management system. While the phrase "just in time" may evoke shades of slap-dash work and cut corners, JiTT pedagogy is just the opposite. It helps students to view learning as a process that takes time, introspection, and persistence.

Students who experience JiTT come to class better prepared, and report that it helps to focus and organize their out-of-class studying. Their responses to JiTT questions make gaps in their learning visible to the teacher prior to class, enabling him or her to address learning gaps while the material is still fresh in students' minds—hence the label "just in time."

JiTT questions differ from traditional homework problems in being designed not only to build cognitive skills, but also to help students confront misconceptions, make connections to previous knowledge, and develop metacognitive thinking practices. Students consequently spend more time on course concepts and ideas, but also read their textbooks in ways that result in more effective and deeper learning. Starting the class with students' work also dramatically changes the classroom-learning environment, creating greater student engagement.